The Himalayan Masters

A Living Tradition

The Himalayan Masters

A Living Tradition

PANDIT RAJMANI TIGUNAIT, PhD

HONESDALE, PENNSYLVANIA USA

When we venture into unknown territory, it is reassuring to have a guide. This is what a spiritual lineage offers us. As questions arise and we encounter obstacles along the way, we can turn to those who have gone before us for inspiration and guidance. *The Himalayan Masters: A Living Tradition* is a collection of stories about the great sages from the Himalayan tradition, beginning with the Vedic seers and continuing to modern times. These sages struggled with the same issues that we all struggle with. And as they overcame the obstacles that stood between them and Self-realization, they mapped the way for those who would follow after them. Passing on the teachings from generation to generation, these sages help lead aspirants to the highest reality.

Each of the stories in this book carries a unique message that will inspire seekers of every level, for they show how even these great realized beings had their moments of doubt and despair—and overcame them. There was Narada, who taught others the art of happiness, only to realize that he was not happy himself. Prince Rama fell into a deep depression and wandered for years in search of inner peace. Parashurama, a great warrior, was consumed with frustration, feeling totally dejected and hopeless. Vidyaranya Yati wondered what was wrong with him because he had not gained direct experience of the truth after more than eighty years of intense practice. Madhusudana Sarasvati, a brilliant philosopher of non-dualism, felt empty inside, and secretly yearned to experience what the devotees did. And Swami Rama kept breaking his practice because he could not always control his anger.

These weary travelers each found the help of a guide who clarified their confusion and inspired them to continue on their spiritual quest. Systematically, step by step, the masters explained how to overcome the obstacles that stand in the way. Be patient, they would say. Train your body, mind, and senses, have faith, study the scriptures, seek the company of the wise, practice non-attachment, meditate. Make all possible effort, and then surrender to divine will. Embrace each moment as it presents itself, seeing it as an opportunity to expand your awareness, until you are fully opened and prepared. Then, when you least expect it, grace will dawn and you will experience oneness with the Divine.

Eventually each of these seekers became a channel through which the ancient teachings flowed, recast to apply to the time and place in which they were given. For me, Swami Rama was that channel. When I first met him in 1978, I knew nothing about the tradition of the Himalayan masters, or the universal teachings of the Vedic lineage they have handed down over the ages. All I knew was that when I was around him, I felt a sense of deep stillness and peace. And as I listened to him lecture and watched him with his students, I knew in my heart that I had found my teacher.

Swamiji cared a great deal about his students and gave us everything he could. For twenty-five years he taught tirelessly, both here and abroad. And no matter what the topic of his lecture, he would always stress the same basic points: "Sit with your head, neck, and trunk straight. Breathe diaphragmatically. Discipline your body, mind, and senses. Learn to know yourself on every level. Be happy. Grease your actions with love. Do not be attached to the fruits of your actions. Practice, practice, practice."

While we clamored for advanced practices, he kept teaching us he same basics, year after year, because he knew that mastering these basics *was* advanced practice. And those who understood knew that the real teachings were given in silence.

Swamiji guided and counseled us in many ways—at times he was gentle and loving, at times stern and aloof. And he had a mischievous childlike side that enjoyed joking and playing with us. Those who wanted to get closer to him, however, soon found out it was like dancing with fire. The closer they got, the hotter the blaze. He was a practical teacher, who created situations to make students learn to think for themselves—and the experience was not always pleasant. Swamiji did not want us to be dependent on anyone or anything external, including him. He encouraged us to go within—to connect with our inner truth. "Meditation," he would say, "can give you that which nothing else can give you; it introduces you to yourself."

He constantly reminded us that we were merely guests passing through this transitory world. We should enjoy it, he insisted, without forgetting that the true purpose of life is to return to our eternal home. Human life, he would say, is a gift, and we should not squander this marvelous opportunity to realize our divine nature.

Whenever we asked Swamiji what we could do for him, he would smile gently and say, "Be happy." For him the way to happiness was through selfless service—by "giving, giving, giving, without expecting anything in return." He admitted that this is a taste that needs to be cultivated, but once we do, he would say, we will drink from the fountain of inner joy.

No matter how much Swamiji gave of himself, he would never take credit for what he did. He told us repeatedly that the knowledge he brought with him had been filtered down to the present through a long line of realized sages. Their ancient teachings are a lear stream of revealed truth that pours ongoing wisdom into the minds and hearts of sincere students. Swamiji's teachings are a modern-day link to this great tradition.

It is this rich heritage that moved Pandit Rajmani Tigunait to write *The Himalayan Masters: A Living Tradition.* He wanted Western students to understand the true teachings of yoga, and to be aware of the vast storehouse of practical knowledge and guidance that is available to spiritual seekers. In the West, yoga has too often been reduced to its physical component—to a series of movements and postures that enhance our physical health and well-being. But the underlying philosophy of yoga is far broader and more profound; it encompasses a holistic approach that creates harmony and balance for body, mind, and spirit on all levels. In this inspiring selection of stories and teachings, Pandit Tigunait gives us a glimpse of the perennial wisdom of the hundreds of sages in the lineage of the Himalayan tradition, and shows us how these teachings are as relevant today as they were thousands of years ago.

The guides are there, waiting to help us. All we have to do is practice, practice, practice.

Irene Petryszak
Chairman, Himalayan Institute

The tradition of the Himalayan sages is an unbroken chain that extends for thousands of years, a living tradition that still exists today undisturbed by the passage of time. This tradition is not concerned with teachings that apply only to a particular era of history or geographical region of the world—its entire emphasis is on the experience of that truth which is eternal and universal. To realize this truth is the highest goal of existence, although at different times and places, different terms have been used to describe it.

Even though the history of this ancient tradition remains shrouded in mystery, it is helpful for modern students to understand it and the lineage of sages who have carried on the teachings. But in seeking to study the tradition, students, no matter how sincere, are at a disadvantage. Many of the ancient texts do not exist in translation, and even when they do, their teachings require clarification and interpretation if they are to provide seekers with any practical guidance.

As Pandit Rajmani Tigunait explains, the unbroken chain of lineage in the Himalayan tradition goes back at least five thousand years (although Shankaracharya, the great philosopher and yogi, formally established the tradition twelve hundred years ago). The sages passed their teachings on orally, each sage transmitting this knowledge directly to students who were prepared to receive it.

The *Vedas* are the sacred texts that contain the wisdom of these ancient sages. In fact, they are the oldest scriptures in the library of humanity. The sages, however, did not create the teachings of the *Vedas*—they are considered to be revealed teachings received intuitively by these great teachers in the depths of their meditative experiences.

Vedanta, which is the essence, or culmination, of the *Vedas*, describes truth as non-dualistic and absolute, and later, sages elaborated on the content of the *Vedas* in the literature known as the *Upanishads*. But even these scriptures require interpretive guidance if they are to be of practical use to modern seekers. In this text, Pandit Tigunait explains the practical implications of these teachings to the modern student.

Meditation is the most powerful tool available to help those who are seeking to attain the experience of truth. It is the technique that helps students go beyond the mire of delusion and conflict that arises in the mind, for truth cannot be known with the mind itself. Many techniques can help students in the preliminary stages of their *sadhana* (spiritual practice), and it is true that for most, preparation of the body, mind, and personality is necessary to allow the full potential of meditation to be achieved. Only by stilling the mind and the senses and by learning to go beyond them can one know truth. Ultimately, meditation is the most important and vital tool needed to attain that goal, and those who sincerely seek to make progress should make certain that they are engaged in an authentic process of meditation, taught by a genuine teacher who can help them with their questions. In other books, the basic techniques of meditation and the steps necessary for deepening it are discussed. Here Pandit Tigunait addresses those who are already embarked on the path of meditation and who want to further develop their understanding of the tradition.

Students of meditation will find that many questions arise as they pursue this goal. Here they can call upon those who have gone before them on the path, and this will help them make the connection with the teacher within. I know that those who study and follow the guidance given in this book will receive help in deepening their meditation and coming closer to the attainment of truth. As Pandit Tigunait reminds them, "The light of eternity dwells within [the human body]. By knowing the systematic yogic methods of penetrating our inner being, it is possible to reach the innermost core of this temple and experience the bliss that lies within." May all who read this important book make progress on their spiritual journey.

THE HIMALAYAN TRADITION

At first glance there seem to be many separate yoga traditions, but in reality there is only one: the tradition that includes all and excludes none, the tradition of the highest truth. This truth is not influenced by time and place, nationality, or race. It is eternal. It remains undisturbed and independent of the whims of society and its transient fashions. It is without boundaries or limitations, and it is not confined to any particular region.

Sincere seekers and teachers in this tradition are not bound by limitations of nationality or geography, or by the fetters of personal ego, ignorance, attachment, aversion, or fear. In this light the tradition of the Himalayan masters is not so much about a geographical location as it is about the heights of spiritual wisdom everywhere.

Our best modern-day scientists and engineers have designed machines to examine all aspects of the external world, from the smallest microbes to distant galaxies, seeking to discover the secrets of the universe. In millennia past, great spiritual researchers focused the power and creativity of their minds on the inner space of their own beings, seeking to discover the full potential of human nature. By using their finely trained, disciplined, and concentrated minds as their tool of exploration, they made their discoveries in the laboratories of their own bodies and minds.

Human civilization is ancient, far older than any recorded history, and it has passed through many cycles of development and decline. Even the oral tradition gives us only sketchy information about the chronological time when these sages lived and began their work. For example, Shankaracharya, the great yogi and philosopher, formally established the tradition of the Himalayan masters twelve hundred years ago. But the written record of this tradition first appears much earlier in the Vedic literature. The *Chhandogya Upanishad,* compiled in approximately 900 B.C., records more than sixty generations in an unbroken lineage of sages. So even if we assign only twenty-five years to each generation, this would take us back to the year 2400 B.C. But according to the oral tradition, the history of the lineage dates back at least five thousand years and perhaps more than ten thousand.

The lineage of the Himalayan sages is not known precisely, especially in its earliest stages. And some of the ancient masters taught so many different disciplines to students over such a long span of time and have been credited with such extraordinary spiritual wisdom and power that it is difficult to believe they were even living human beings. But they were. Freethinkers and explorers of the highest truth, they were the architects of human civilization. The philosophers, saints, and yogis who came later built upon their blueprint of spirituality.

The Himalayan region seems to have had a more moderate climate thousands of years ago than it does today, and this supplied the ancient sage-scientists with a perfect setting in which to carry out their experiments. The natural serenity of the mountains, the moderate temperatures, clean water, edible roots, fruit-laden trees, and comfortable dwellings far removed from worldly noise and distractions gave them the environment they needed for the subtle practices that made their discoveries possible. And there are hundreds of shrines and holy places throughout the Himalayas that are dedicated to the memory of these sages and to the saints and adepts who lived there after them. Even now, as in the past, yogis who belong to the Himalayan tradition go to this region for their higher training. If they are well prepared, they are able to join the cave monasteries hidden deep in the Himalayan peaks, where they receive advanced instruction and attain the highest state of spiritual illumination. Mere curiosity is not enough to enable outsiders to find these caves: they have their own kind of subtle fences that prevent half-hearted seekers from reaching them. The charms and temptations of the world, the comfort-oriented tendencies of the mind, and ultimately, the lack of strong inspiration serve to screen would-be students, and only a fortunate few qualify to study and practice with the sages.

The mountains cannot support large numbers of people, so many of the problems related to overpopulation (such as possessiveness, greed, theft, violence, and fear) are virtually unknown there. And the sages have used the hardships of mountain life to cultivate such spiritual virtues as non-possessiveness, generosity, love, and fearlessness.

This is the Himalayan way of life, and it has remained unchanged to this day. Villagers find happiness in sharing their limited resources with strangers. In fact, in their simplicity, purity, and innocence, they do not consider anyone to be a stranger. Everyone who arrives at their door, no matter how unexpectedly, is treated as a guest. It is this attitude that makes it possible for yogis to survive in the mountains without carrying the burden of worldly possessions.

The ancient scriptures are filled with descriptions of these peaceful places, but they are not found just in the Himalayas. Many other mountain ranges and hills—such as the Vindhya Mountains, which stretch from central India all the way to the southern peninsula—also serve as havens for spiritual seekers and teachers. Despite the changing weather patterns during the past millennia that have made living conditions harsher than they were in earlier times, places such as Chitrakut in the northern Vindhya range,

Nasik and Amarakantak in central India, Girnar near the west coast in Gujarat, and Arunachala in the south are still spiritually active centers. Ultimately, however, these sites are connected to the cave monasteries in the Himalayas. Students from these centers are often sent to the caves for higher training, and sometimes adepts from the cave monasteries travel to these places to guide the students there.

From a literary point of view, the tradition of the Himalayan masters was first expounded in the *Vedas,* then gradually evolved through the development of the *Upanishads* and the *Puranas,* and finally formed the basis of the saintly literature written in the regional languages of India. Therefore, in essence, the tradition of the Himalayan masters is the tradition of the Vedic sages.

Both oral and literary sources say that Narayana, one of the immortal, primordial sages, is the founder of the Himalayan tradition. They say that he transcends the confines of our individual consciousness and is one with universal consciousness and that, as such, he is totally free of ignorance, ego, attachment, aversion, and fear. In him lies the seed of omniscience. This enlightened soul is also free from the karmas, the fruits of karmas, and all the consequences brought about by the law of karma. The tradition also tells us that Narayana is the pure space of consciousness. Just as the whole world exists in space, yet space remains untouched by the world, so all other sages, adepts, and seekers dwell in Narayana and receive guidance from him, yet Narayana remains unaffected by this. Because of his elevated spiritual awareness, the tradition identifies him with God, for the depth of spiritual awareness he dwells in is completely beyond the realm of time and space. It can be said, therefore, that Narayana is without a beginning and without an end. He existed and still exists, although no one knows whether or not he was ever born.

But we are accustomed to locating an object, a person, a tradition, or an institution in space and time, and so it is difficult to understand that a figure such as Narayana, and a tradition that "begins" with him, is beginningless. We are used to the concept of "the beginning of creation" and "the end of creation," and we assume that anything that exists must have had a beginning. That is why we think of Narayana, who may well be an actual person, as a mythological figure. But a peak named after him stands amid the majesty of the Himalayas. And according to tradition, the famous shrine of Badrinath is the site of his ashram. The spiritual practices he undertook while he lived in this ashram and the knowledge he imparted to numberless saints and sages are chronicled in the Vedic, tantric, and epic literature of India.

Sanatkumara is another sage who holds an exalted place in the history of the Himalayan masters. According to some sources, he and his three brothers (Sanaka, Sanandana, and Sanatsujata) are the sons of Brahma, the Creator. According to other sources they are the offspring of a couple named Ahimsa and Dharma. But whatever his parentage, Sanatkumara appears in the vast body of spiritual literature teaching the wisdom of the *Vedas,* the *Upanishads,* yoga, and tantra. The lineage of the Himalayan tradition begins with this master and is followed in an unbroken line by Vashishtha, Shakti, Parashara, Vyasa, Shuka Deva, Gaudapada, Govindapada, and Shankaracharya.

This list is not exhaustive; there were many other great saints and sages between Sanatkumara and Shankaracharya, but it is difficult to determine the exact order of their appearance. Among them are Atharava, Angiras, Dakshinamurti, Chyavana, Dadhichi, Dattatreya, Hayagriva, Parashurama, and Haritayana. These are the seers of the mantras and the teachers of spiritual sciences such as *agni vidya,* the science of the spiritual sun; *chandra vidya,* the science of the spiritual moon; *deha vijñana,* the science pertaining to the subtle mysteries of the body; and *svara vijñana,* the science of breath.

The breadth and scope of the spiritual literature that issued from these sages is enormous, and in preparing the present volume we were forced to be extremely selective. Finally, after careful deliberation we elected to include only the eight masters whose teachings have the most direct bearing on the questions that confront most serious seekers today. Accordingly this volume contains chapters on Sanatkumara, Vashishtha, Dattatreya, Parashurama, and Shankaracharya, five masters who either were authors themselves or had students who recorded their teachings. However, Vyasa, who is the most famous of all the ancient masters, was not included, because his work is widely available. And many of the other great sages in this lineage, such as Atharava and Angiras, were also excluded because they contributed mainly to the esoteric aspect of yogic literature and their teachings are of interest only to those who are wholeheartedly dedicated to mysticism. Finally, even though the last three masters included in this volume—Vidyaranya Yati, Madhusudana Sarasvati, and Swami Rama—are considerably more modern, they represent different facets of the lineage that began with Shankaracharya and continues in a pure form until this day.

The *Vedas* and the *Upanishads* are the earliest written sources of the Himalayan tradition. Indeed, the *Vedas* are the oldest spiritual scriptures in the library of humanity. They are not the works of an ordinary intellect; they are the spontaneous, intuitive revelations that came to the sages in the form of words, and that is why every word and verse in the *Vedas* is called a mantra.

Later on, the sages elaborated on the content of the *Vedas* in the *Upanishads,* where they presented the essence of the *Vedas* and described yogic techniques for studying and practicing the mantras in daily life. Hundreds of *Upanishads* evolved from the *Vedas,* but eleven are considered major: the *Isha, Kena, Katha, Prashna, Mundaka, Mandukya, Chhandogya, Taittiriya, Aitareya, Brihadaranyaka,* and *Shvetashvatara Upanishads.* They all expound the theory of *advaita* (non-dualism)—that there is only one absolute, highest truth without a second—and they all tell aspirants to be aware of that truth derstand that a figure such as Narayana, and a tradition that "begins" with him, is beginningless. We are used to the concept of "the beginning of creation" and "the end of creation," and we assume that anything that exists must have had a beginning. That is why we think of Narayana, who may well be an actual person, as a mythological figure. But a peak named after him stands amid the majesty of the Himalayas. And according to tradition, the famous shrine of Badrinath is the site of his ashram. The spiritual practices he undertook while he lived in this ashram and the knowledge he imparted to numberless saints and sages are chronicled in the Vedic, tantric, and epic literature of India.

Sanatkumara is another sage who holds an exalted place in the history of the Himalayan masters. According to some sources, he and his three brothers (Sanaka, Sanandana, and Sanatsujata) are the sons of Brahma, the Creator. According to other sources they are the offspring of a couple named Ahimsa and Dharma. But whatever his parentage, Sanatkumara appears in the vast body of spiritual literature teaching the wisdom of the *Vedas*, the *Upanishads*, yoga, and tantra. The lineage of the Himalayan tradition begins with this master and is followed in an unbroken line by Vashishtha, Shakti, Parashara, Vyasa, Shuka Deva, Gaudapada, Govindapada, and Shankaracharya.

This list is not exhaustive; there were many other great saints and sages between Sanatkumara and Shankaracharya, but it is difficult to determine the exact order of their appearance. Among them are Atharava, Angiras, Dakshinamurti, Chyavana, Dadhichi, Dattatreya, Hayagriva, Parashurama, and Haritayana. These are the seers of the mantras and the teachers of spiritual sciences such as *agni vidya*, the science of the spiritual sun; *chandra vidya*, the science of the spiritual moon; *deha vijñana*, the science pertaining to the subtle mysteries of the body; and *svara vijñana*, the science of breath.

The breadth and scope of the spiritual literature that issued from these sages is enormous, and in preparing the present volume we were forced to be extremely selective. Finally, after careful deliberation we elected to include only the eight masters whose teachings have the most direct bearing on the questions that confront most serious seekers today. Accordingly this volume contains chapters on Sanatkumara, Vashishtha, Dattatreya, Parashurama, and Shankaracharya, five masters who either were authors themselves or had students who recorded their teachings. However, Vyasa, who is the most famous of all the ancient masters, was not included, because his work is widely available. And many of the other great sages in this lineage, such as Atharava and Angiras, were also excluded because they contributed mainly to the esoteric aspect of yogic literature and their teachings are of interest only to those who are wholeheartedly dedicated to mysticism. Finally, even though the last three masters included in this volume—Vidyaranya Yati, Madhusudana Sarasvati, and Swami Rama—are considerably more modern, they represent different facets of the lineage that began with Shankaracharya and continues in a pure form until this day.

The *Vedas* and the *Upanishads* are the earliest written sources of the Himalayan tradition. Indeed, the *Vedas* are the oldest spiritual scriptures in the library of humanity. They are not the works of an ordinary intellect; they are the spontaneous, intuitive revelations that came to the sages in the form of words, and that is why every word and verse in the *Vedas* is called a mantra.

Later on, the sages elaborated on the content of the *Vedas* in the *Upanishads,* where they presented the essence of the *Vedas* and described yogic techniques for studying and practicing the mantras in daily life. Hundreds of *Upanishads* evolved from the *Vedas,* but eleven are considered major: the *Isha, Kena, Katha, Prashna, Mundaka, Mandukya, Chhandogya, Taittiriya, Aitareya, Brihadaranyaka,* and *Shvetashvatara Upanishads*. They all expound the theory of *advaita* (non-dualism)—that there is only one absolute, highest truth without a second—and they all tell aspirants to be aware of that truth and aspire to attain it while they experience the vicissitudes of life. In its opening verses the *Isha Upanishad* conveys the message of the Vedic seers in this way:

This whole world has evolved from one absolute truth: Isha. The whole world, even after its manifestation, dwells in Isha; all worldly objects are a gift from Isha to human beings. Therefore enjoy the objects of the world, but never get attached to them. Do not covet, do not possess, because nothing belongs to you. While performing your actions, desire to live for one hundred years. Actions you perform while maintaining the awareness of Isha do not bind you.

The *Upanishads* include many references to highly evolved yogic practices, but they are too brief and compact to be understood without the help of an experienced master. The contemplative aspects of the teachings, however, are so clear and systematic that the eleven major *Upanishads* have become a sourcebook for the many different philosophical systems and contemplative schools of Indian spirituality.

The higher disciplines of yoga and meditation, those that are mentioned only fleetingly in the *Vedas* and *Upanishads*, are fully explained in another group of texts known as the *Tantras* or *Agamas*. In these texts, however, the contents are presented in such a highly symbolic and mystical language that they are incomprehensible to the uninitiated. Thus if aspirants are to comprehend the true intent of tantric texts, they must be instructed directly by a master.

The outstanding tantric texts of the Himalayan tradition are *Sanaka Samhita, Sanandana Samhita, Sanatkumara Samhita, Vashishtha Samhita,* and *Sukha Samhita.* Unfortunately, none of these scriptures exist today. However, thousands of tantric scriptures that are based on them do exist, the most important of which are *Parashurama Kalpa Sutra, Tripura Rahasya, Nitya Sodashikarnava,*

Rudrayamala, and *Saundaryalahari* (along with its forty-one commentaries). But except for *Tripura Rahasya* and *Saundaryalahari,* none have been translated into English.

In addition to the Vedic and tantric texts there is a third body of literature that stems from the Himalayan tradition: the *Puranas.* These texts take the form of stories, so their teachings are simpler and easier to comprehend than the teachings in the Vedic and tantric literature. The drawback, however, is that the content is diluted. The reader finds the point of the narrative only after wading through many long and involved stories. And because the stories were told and retold and presented in different ways for different audiences, elaborations and distortions were inevitable. In other words, the *Puranas* are like a great ocean. In order to retrieve the pearls from it, a student must first figure out where to dive, and then learn to dive deep.

In order to meet the needs of seekers in different times and at different places, the sages imparted many levels of knowledge, and they did so in a variety of idioms. The result is that there are thousands of texts. Some teach a dualistic philosophy of life, some are non-dualistic; some teach a materialistic worldview, some are completely spiritual; some advocate a family-oriented lifestyle, others stress ascetic practices. Keeping in mind both the vastness of the body of this spiritual literature and the depth of the sages' knowledge, no one can ever claim with authority that "this and this alone is what the sages teach." In order to avoid the mistake of confining teachings to a narrow framework, it is helpful to remember the following story about Buddha and his students:

> Buddha's students used to quarrel among themselves, each claiming that what he had learned from the master was the only true teaching. So once, when Buddha was walking through the forest with his students, he picked up a handful of leaves and asked, "Does my hand contain more

leaves than there are in the rest of the forest?"

"No," the students replied. "It's obvious that you have only a few leaves in your hand, while the leaves in the forest are innumerable."

"So it is with the knowledge that I have imparted to a few students," Buddha replied. "I know much more than I have taught."

Like Buddha, the sages of the *Upanishads* warn their students: "Practice only those teachings that are meaningful to you at this particular stage of your development. Leave the rest for further study and contemplation. In time, you may come to know their importance and come to understand them."

At the heart of the Himalayan tradition, however, is advaita, the revelation that there is only one absolute, non-dual truth. Acquiring this knowledge is like climbing the highest peak of a mountain and seeing the panorama below. All the sights that were visible from the lower elevations are included in this view, but from the summit they do not look like they did when the viewer was standing in the valley or partway up the mountain. So it is with the spiritual quest. At different stages of spiritual unfoldment, different revelations are valid and appropriate.

From a practical standpoint, however, all the sages—regardless of which philosophy they teach or which aspect of truth they expound—share common, basic values.

Ahimsa (non-violence) is the backbone of spirituality. It is humankind's highest dharma (duty). The Sanskrit phrase for this is *ahimsa paramo dharmah*. Violence is the root of all vices, the sages tell us, because all species—human and non-human—are naturally inclined to peace and happiness; no one wants to be miserable. Therefore, causing pain to yourself or others violates both the law of nature and divine law.

Wherever there is conflict between ahimsa and our personal cultural values, customs, and religious practices, ahimsa must be preserved. It can help resolve conflicts between religions and cultures, and is the only way to bring humanity into one fold and open the eyes of aspirants to the manifestation of the one truth in all that exists.

To practice ahimsa, however, we must create a healthy lifestyle that does not disturb our own well-being, that of our communities, or that of society as a whole *(acharah prathamo dharmah)*. And it is crucial to observe the basic guidelines for healthy living *(acharah)*—cleanliness and purity—if we are to create a healthy environment for our own growth, the growth of others, and the welfare of future generations. What is more, these guidelines must be observed on all levels of existence—physical, verbal, and mental.

The human body, the sages tell us, is the living shrine of the Divine *(deho devalayah proktah)*. The light of eternity dwells within it. By knowing the systematic yogic methods of penetrating our inner being, it is possible to reach the innermost core of this temple and experience the bliss that lies within. To be born as a human is a great opportunity, the sages say. Failing to attain the highest realization before dropping the body is the greatest loss we can experience.

The physical body is the basic vehicle for reaching the goal of life's journey. It is the primary means for practicing dharma *(shariram adyam khalu dharamsadhanam)*. A sound mind dwells in a healthy body; an unhealthy body can create innumerable impediments. Those whose time and energy are consumed with solving problems created by the body have little opportunity to explore the higher levels of truth, and for this reason the lifestyle and practices that help maintain a healthy body are an integral part of *sadhana* (spiritual practice).

By practicing physical cleanliness we ensure our own good health and the purity of our environment. The same is true in the verbal realm. The pollution we create by telling lies and speaking negatively is far more injurious and lasting than the problems we cause by failing to keep our body or our physical environment clean. In turn, the damage caused by mental impurity—anger, hatred, jealousy, and greed—is far more injurious and long-lasting than the damage caused by verbal impurity. That is why all of the sages speak with one voice when they stress the importance of eating pure, fresh food, breathing fresh air, speaking the truth, and maintaining purity of thought. This constitutes a human being's basic dharma.

The Himalayan masters also say that we must be fearless. On the most obvious level fear springs from the desire for self-preservation, but on a deeper level fear springs from a sense of aloneness. No matter how many systems of philosophy and psychology we follow, fear of death cannot be overcome unless we realize our unity with the one, all-embracing, absolute, non-dual truth. As long as we perceive ourselves as individuals, we will be afraid of losing that identity.

The ego is the source of the sense of individuality. It is aware that it is a false self, but it does not want to accept this fact, and thus it creates conflict and fear. But the knowledge of the absolute truth and our oneness with it is the ground on which fear vanishes completely *(dvaitad vai bhayam bhavati advaitad vai amritah bhavanti)*. That is the goal of sadhana. The sages equate this state with immortality. External peace manifests from internal peace *(vyakter vai virat; antas shanter bahis shantih)*.

Everyone is a vessel of light, the sages say, and if humankind is to live in peace and harmony this light must radiate from each of us. The relationship between individuals and humanity is like the relationship between the trees and the forest. Just as a large group of trees becomes a forest, so do individuals form families, communities, societies, and humanity.

The health of the forest deteriorates when individual trees are diseased. By the same token, it is impossible to have a healthy society unless the individuals who make up that society are healthy. As the individual's quality of life improves, so does society's quality of life. And just as a prosperous society supplies the means for living comfortably, so do people who are comfortable have a better chance of exploring and understanding the subtle truths of life. This entire cycle of spiritual unfoldment begins and ends with the individual.

All of the ethical, moral, and social values of the sages are based on one spiritual truth: There is only one Brahman, without a second *(eko Brahma dvitiyo nasti)*. Like different steps on a ladder, all the paths of yoga gradually lead to this truth *(tadunmukhah sarvapanthanah sopanavata)*. But in climbing toward the goal, it is important to know where you are on the ladder. Then you must stand firm in your own sadhana without judging whether or not your path is higher or lower, superior or inferior, to others. This will help you rise above seeming contradictions among the different paths.

To experience the Atman—the true Self—within is immortality *(atmanyevatmanam nivodhata tadeva amaratvam)*. This is the sages' most important message; it is the highest truth. But searching for this truth in the external world is a waste of time and the source of endless misery. If you cannot find your Self wherever you are, then certainly you cannot find your Self anywhere else. Not finding your Self is called death; finding your Self is called immortality.

The highest truth is one, but its faces are many; so the sages have revealed its different faces at different times and described it from different viewpoints. And just as different faces of the truth are equally valid and authentic, so are the different teachings. The chapters that follow present the faces of truth that are most relevant to seekers in the present age.

SANATKUMARA

The teachings of the great sage Sanatkumara have been preserved in a number of works, among them the *Chhandogya Upanishad,* the *Mahabharata,* the *Harivamsa Purana,* the *Vamana Purana,* the *Skanda Purana,* the *Brahmanda Purana,* and the *Mahatymya Khanda* of *Tripura Rahasya.* The multi-volume publication *Kalyana* (which has not been translated into English) also contains information about him. The following sampling of Sanatkumara's teachings is taken primarily from the *Chhandogya Upanishad.*

Once there was a learned yogi named Narada. In addition to his knowledge of the scriptures he was an expert in philosophy, history, grammar, mathematics, economics, ethics, logic, mythology, astrology, astronomy, medicine, and a host of other disciplines. All in all he had mastered sixty-four different branches of art and science. His students revered him for his knowledge, and he was recognized everywhere as a teacher of the highest wisdom.

But one day he realized that even though he taught others the art of happiness, he wasn't truly happy himself. He began to have second thoughts about his accomplishments, and as he pondered this, he began to reevaluate his way of life as well as his wisdom. Finally after much thought Narada came to the conclusion that the methods he taught for removing frustration, dejection, depression, and loneliness could not help students if they did not also help the teacher. And he definitely was not happy, despite his abundant knowledge. And what of others whose knowledge was much more limited than his? How could they be happy? He began to wonder if anyone in the world was happy.

The more he thought about it, the more determined he became to find true happiness, so he handed over all his responsibilities to his senior students and set out on this quest. He was greeted with honor wherever he went, but no one took him seriously when he spoke of his search and expressed his doubts. Those whose advice he sought thought he was simply being humble, so no one offered him guidance.

Finally, Narada found Sanatkumara, and that great sage agreed to help him. Sanatkumara asked him what he had already learned, and Narada went over the long list of arts and sciences he had mastered. When he had finished, the following dialogue transpired.

S a n a t k u m a r a : You know so much, and still you are not happy.

N a r a d a : My knowledge has not brought me peace or joy. It does not help me overcome my fear of death. I am tired of knowing things and at the same time drowning in misery. Please take me beyond knowing, to where I may find freedom. Everything I have learned so far, everything I have gained through years of arduous study, is only a means of exercising my skills or gaining worldly recognition. How can this have any real value, considering that I will lose it at death and have to start all over again in the next lifetime?

S a n a t k u m a r a : The problem is that you confuse true knowledge, which is gained directly from within, with mere information, which is gained through words and sentences. All the branches of art and science that you have mastered are simply collections of words—they have no substance. Your knowledge of these disciplines has given you the means for maintaining your existence on this earthly plane; this is why most people master these subjects, even though what they are teaching and learning fails to bring them true happiness.

Meanwhile the book of life remains unread. The part of you that is destined to unveil the mystery of life prompts you to open this book and read attentively. But while you are engaged in mundane activities you are ignoring its call, the call of the soul, with its constant reminder of the highest truth. Thus you create a ground for inner conflict, and this results in frustration and destroys your peace and happiness.

You may be able to hide yourself from the rest of the world, but you cannot conceal yourself from yourself, from your soul. The only way to achieve real peace and happiness is to know yourself at every level of your being.

N a r a d a : How can I do that? How can I know myself at every level?

S a n a t k u m a r a : Your speech is a reflection of your thoughts, and your inner life is created by the way you think. Speech is the means through which the mind expresses itself; so if you want to know your inner life, first examine your speech. The more you study it, the more the contents of your mind are revealed. Study the connection between speech and mind.

You can attain some degree of control over your speech by observing silence, but this will not bring you peace. In order to attain that, you must work systematically. First, bring peace to your tongue. This means speaking sweetly and making sure that you do not harm either yourself or others through your speech. Then avoid meaningless talk. Once the disturbance at the level of speech is quieted, however, you will notice unexpected turbulence in the mind.

Mind is subtler than speech, so the next step is to study your mind. Contemplate on what you think, why you think it, and how your thoughts affect your speech and actions. If you cannot quiet the mental noise, then fill your mind with the awareness of

Brahman, the highest truth. Then you will notice an even subtler force, called *sankalpa* [determination]. It is only at your behest that your mind thinks; it cannot think unless you decide that it will, and only when your mind thinks do words come forth. Thus your determination, which is a subtle desire springing from the core of your being, is the driving force behind the activities of your mind.

N a r a d a :   If sankalpa is even more subtle than the mind, then why can't we make our mind do what we want it to do? It seems to me that we have very little control over our sankalpa and that the mind's activities go unchecked.

S a n a t k u m a r a :   You are right, Narada. Your determination is affected by your *samskaras* [the subtle impressions of the past] and by the thoughts, speech, and actions you have stored in the *chitta* [the mindfield]. But you have forgotten these things, as well as the place where you stored them, and they have become unconscious. Their storehouse is the unconscious mind, and the material stored there affects the power of your determination without your being aware of it. Thus your sankalpa has lost control over the conscious part of the mind. That is why, for example, you sometimes think thoughts you don't want to think, speak words you don't wish to speak, postpone certain thoughts or actions, and perform actions you don't want to perform. All this is because of the subtle impressions of the past that are stored in the unconscious mind and lie dormant there. Unless something awakens them, they have no power to affect either your determination or your conscious mind.

N a r a d a :   Is there any rule governing how and when the subtle impressions of the past arise?

S a n a t k u m a r a :   The law is simple: Similar attracts similar. Nothing is totally unconscious. It is contemplation, a facet of your conscious thinking, that triggers corresponding samskaras. Contemplation awakens these subtle impressions, which in turn affect your sankalpa and your conscious mind as well as your speech and action. Contemplation also prevents the unconscious mind from controlling the conscious mind. But it is your *sankalpa shakti* [the power of determination] that makes contemplation effective. It is more powerful than the unconscious mind.

For a novice, it is hard to work at this level, because even though the force of contemplation triggers the power of determination and reaches the conscious mind, it awakens unconscious material as well, and this can include the negative samskaras.

Therefore, Narada, because it is hard to penetrate these subtle layers of our being in the early stages of our sadhana, from the very beginning it is advisable to contemplate on the one principle that is more powerful than the negative samskaras. Fill your contemplation with the highest truth, Brahman-consciousness, while you simultaneously work toward self-transformation and self-improvement.

In other words, in the beginning you should maintain Brahman-consciousness by keeping the highest goal in mind throughout your study of the scriptures, throughout your discourses, and in your reasoning. In that way the lower knowledge you gain through worldly sources becomes a means of gaining knowledge of the highest truth. I am not speaking of intellectual knowledge but of self-revealed, intuitive knowledge, which does not come from books, discourses, or reasoning.

N a r a d a : All these years I have believed that the way I was studying and teaching was a definite method of *svadhyaya* [self-study].

S a n a t k u m a r a : Your studies and teaching activities were only a means of entertaining yourself, of gaining recognition, of finding intellectual satisfaction, and of keeping yourself busy and earning a living. Such studying and teaching is mere action. No one can achieve freedom through action alone.

N a r a d a : Should I abandon all these actions, then? Aren't they better than many other actions? Aren't they better than not performing any actions at all?

S a n a t k u m a r a : That's not the point, Narada. It's a matter of gathering your courage and tapping your inner strength. Your resolve to act works only if it is accompanied by the inner strength that comes not from the surface of your mind or from your intellect but from the depth of your soul, from *shakti,* the divine force that is unalloyed. Without shakti, knowledge of action and the resolve to act will come to nothing.

So make your knowledge functional. Unless it is, knowledge is a burden. Knowledge that doesn't wake you up and make you move forward is dead. It must be active and vibrant, for it is from the womb of active knowledge that the power of action is born. Active knowledge takes life from *ichccha shakti* [the unrestricted power of will], which is intrinsic to the highest truth. Ichccha shakti is also *kama kala* [initial, or primordial, divine desire]. Therefore, to make your knowledge active and vibrant you must meditate and thereby unfold the supreme power of will within. The power of will, the power of knowledge, and the power of action reinforce one another.

N a r a d a : How can I understand the nature of shakti and unfold that force within?

S a n a t k u m a r a : Shakti is the primordial, divine life-force. It manifests in everything you perceive. Before a living organism evolves, something must exist to sustain it—first comes the nourishment, then the organism. The life-force is in both. Thus the life-force is both consumer and consumed. Unless you know the intrinsic nature of the life-force within you and within the objects that nourish you, you will live with the fear that you will not be able to sustain your own life. Unless you know who the consumer is and who is being consumed, you will never overcome the fear of death.

There are two forms of fear: the fear of not having enough to maintain yourself, and the fear of being consumed by the objects you possess. In either case you remain involved with objects—either in acquiring those that make you feel secure, or in ridding yourself of those that threaten you.

But it is not enough to know that you need solid food, water, light, heat, and air to live. You must also know what it is that you receive from these things, how the life-force is different from these things, and why the life-force is supplied through them. Ultimately, you need to know under what conditions you receive and assimilate —or fail to receive and assimilate—the life-force from these substances. At this point, Narada, the inquiry moves across the boundary of physics and into the realm of metaphysics, or even into pure spiritual science. The nature and structure of the universe, its functioning forces, and its constituent components are thoroughly studied in the science of *Sri Vidya*.

19

Sanatkumara explains the science of *Sri Vidya* in the *Sanatkumara Samhita*. Here the sage leads Narada in a step-by-step dialogue, unveiling the mysteries of the power of memory and its connection with the principles of hope, pranic energy, the power of decisiveness, faith, conviction, and, ultimately, happiness. Sanatkumara stresses that true happiness cannot be limited by time, space, and causation. It cannot be compared with any experience at all. It cannot be categorized as being "less" or "more," "small" or "big," "short-lived" or "long-lasting." An excerpt from this dialogue follows.

S a n a t k u m a r a : You have come from bliss, Narada, and no matter how deeply you get lost in the world, part of you remains aware of your blissful nature. It is that part which reminds you, from within, to search for and attain eternal, boundless bliss and become one with it.

The urge to attain happiness is the driving force behind all pursuits in life, but the charms and temptations of worldly objects are so strong that you don't remember to turn inward and find the wealth of happiness that lies within yourself. Deep down, however, you miss that happiness, and in order to rid yourself of the feeling of "missingness" you redouble your effort to find happiness in the external world.

For example, before you undertake a task there is the light of hope, and this gives you some degree of joy. You work hard, hoping to find happiness by obtaining objects. But when you obtain them your happiness fades, and soon you are dissatisfied again. So you look for something else. You continue performing actions in the external world with the elusive hope that the next one will make you happy, even though the last one did not.

Every failure is a lesson which teaches you that there is no real happiness in the external world. But your doubt that happiness can be found in the unknown inner realm—possibly at the price of losing the pleasure of the external world—frightens you. And fear and happiness never coexist. So as long as you have no direct experience of the happiness that lies within you, you must trust the experiences of the sages or the testimony of the scriptures and find the courage to turn the mind inward.

This is called "standing on the ground of faith." Before you gain direct experience of the truth within, faith is the only force that can loosen the fetters of desire and attachment to worldly pleasure. Faith is higher knowledge in its own right. It gives you the courage to turn away from the external world and find the truth in the place where all limitation ends.

N a r a d a : In practical terms, how do I begin my search?

S a n a t k u m a r a : You begin with food. Through *ahara shuddhi* [eating pure food] you purify your body. Then, just as your gross body needs solid food to maintain its existence, so does your pranic body need pranic energy. On an even more subtle level, the senses, mind, ego, and intellect all require their own kind of food. *Sattvic* food that is fresh, light, and nutritious, taken in the appropriate quantities, at the right time, and with the right attitude of mind, provides a pure diet. Breathing clean air, with a regulated balance of right- and left-nostril dominance, nourishes the pranic body. Maintaining positive thoughts in a cheerful mind provides nutritious food to the mental body. Constant awareness that anything indicated by the words "my" and "mine" belongs to nature and that anything indicated by "I" is pure consciousness supplies nutritious food to the ego. Purify yourself by maintaining the constant awareness that all objects belong to nature and it is a mistake to identify with them. At the same time, remain aware of your pure existence, consciousness, and bliss.

When you purify your external and internal life by purifying the food you provide to every level of your being, your memory becomes sharp and stable and you begin to glimpse the highest truth, your inner Self. As these glimpses become brighter and steadier, your attachment to worldly objects and your desire for pleasure become thinner and weaker. The weaker your desires and attachments, the greater the illumination of your inner Self. And the greater the light that radiates from within, the brighter you will see yourself both within and without.

By imparting this knowledge, Sanatkumara resolved all Narada's questions and helped him attain freedom from the frustration caused by a sense of "missingness" and loneliness.

Sanatkumara's teachings are documented in the vast literature of the *Upanishads* and *Puranas* as well as in the *Agamas* and *Tantras*. In the more accessible literature, Sanatkumara is portrayed as *paramahansa*, the highest *jñani* (knower of truth), perfectly and eternally established in the principle of *vairagya* (non-attachment). He is known as *brahmarishi* (the knower of Brahman), who guides students who are prepared on the path of knowledge.

On the one hand it is said that Sanatkumara's body is made of pure light and descends into the pure mindfield of yogis, where it imparts the highest wisdom to them. On the other hand, for those who have not reached that high degree of purity (acquired through yoga) and thus are unable to face the brilliance that emanates from his presence, Sanatkumara materializes in human form and guides them lovingly on the path of truth, usually through *bhakti* yoga, the path of devotion. In tantric literature he is the primordial master from whom flows the wisdom of tantra, especially the wisdom of the ten *mahavidyas* (the sublime paths of shakti-oriented tantric practices). In the splendid tree of the tradition of the sages, Sanatkumara is the root; the others are the trunk and the branches.

VASHISHTHA

According to legend, Vashishtha is the son of Brahma, the creator of the universe. It happened like this: Once long ago Brahma looked down at the world and noticed that numberless human souls were living in the darkness of ignorance. Their existence was miserable. Exhausted from the strenuous round of worldly activities, they simply fell asleep at the end of each lifetime, hoping to get some rest and awaken to find their troubles at an end. But that never happened, and they remained caught in an endless cycle of death and rebirth.

Seeing this, Brahma said to himself, "Let me bring forth my beloved son, Vashishtha, who has the wisdom to help these suffering souls."

Instantly Vashishtha emerged, radiant as the midday sun. Bowing his head in reverence, he asked, "What would you have me do, O Creator of the World?"

"Beloved son," Brahma answered, "I command you to descend to the world and live as a human being. Show the path of freedom and enlightenment to those helpless souls who are entangled in the cycle of worldly transmigration."

Vashishtha replied, "But this manifest world, myself included, is part of the divine game. This process of creation and annihilation goes on under the guidance of the supreme force, *maha maya*. The concept of bondage and liberation is illusory; it has no meaning. How can the true essence of the soul ever be bound and miserable?"

With this, Brahma realized that because Vashishtha's perfection and purity had not been compromised by worldly afflictions he did not understand bondage and freedom, pleasure and pain, sorrow and happiness. He was an omniscient soul, able to see the essential nature of omniscience and bliss—his own Self, and the Self of all. And in the light of this omniscience he was unable to see the darkness of ignorance and the misery it caused. Brahma realized that his son's omniscience would have to be taken from him if he was to understand human consciousness and find practical methods for helping humans overcome their pain and misery. With this thought, Brahma spoke: "May you lose your omniscience, my son."

Suddenly Vashishtha did not know who he was. He did not recognize his own father. "Can you tell me who I am?" he had to ask.

"You are Vashishtha, my son."

"Then who are you, sir?"

"I am Brahma, your father, the creator of the universe."

"How unfortunate I am!" Vashishtha cried out. "You say I am your son, and yet I do not know whose son I am. You say you are my father, and yet I do not know in what sense you are my father. I am completely separate from you. I am a human being with none of your qualities or characteristics. Help me, Father. Save me! Let me understand my purpose and how I may accomplish it."

Brahma then explained the nature of ignorance to his son, step by step, and finally reintroduced him to his pure Self, where the seed of omniscience and bliss lies. With that Vashishtha bowed his head humbly and said, "How may I serve you?"

"Go to the Earth, beloved Vashishtha, and teach your fellow beings to recognize and follow the path that best suits them."

That is how the human race came to be blessed with the presence of Vashishtha. According to the scriptures, this sage lived for a

long time. He practiced and taught almost all the spiritual disciplines during his long life's journey. The following episode in his
life describes what peace is and where it can be found.

After teaching and meditating for many years, Vashishtha decided to abandon the rush and roar of the world and find a place
that was absolutely quiet. So he set off for one of the far-distant
galaxies where he was not known. Traveling through the vast abyss
of space, he went past the boundaries of this three-dimensional
world, and there in pure space—far from planets and stars—he
hoped to remain undisturbed. He sat down to begin his meditation.
Soon he went into deep *samadhi* (the state of mind in which there
are no thought constructs).

Several hundred years passed before Vashishtha opened his
eyes. A beautiful young woman was walking toward him. "A living
human being here in empty space? What is this?" he wondered,
amazed.

The young maiden approached, paid homage to him, and
pleaded, "Help me, O son of Brahma."

"Who are you, and what can I do for you?" Vashishtha inquired.

"I am the daughter of the creator of a galaxy. My father will not
allow me to marry, although I am in the full flower of my youth.
Please talk to him; I'm sure he will listen to you. Prevent my youth
from being wasted."

Vashishtha agreed to help her, and when they arrived at her
father's galaxy, its creator came forward and received Vashishtha
respectfully. "Why will you not allow your daughter to marry?"
Vashishtha asked.

Her father replied, "In seven days this entire galaxy and everyone in it, myself included, will be destroyed. I have told my daughter to make the best use of these seven days and attain that
immortal knowledge which remains unaffected by the forces of creation and destruction. Why create a bond for the sake of a pleasure
that is destined to last for only seven days?"

Vashishtha turned to the young woman and said, "Your father is right. Why do you want to concentrate on momentary enjoyment which is bound to end in misery?"

"All living beings adjust their mind and heart to the idea of pleasure and pain," she replied. "The intensity of both longing and fulfillment is qualitatively the same for one whose life lasts only seven days as it is for one whose life spans seven hundred years. How can you apply the same standard of inner happiness and spiritual bliss to an enlightened person like yourself and to someone who is completely affected by the turmoil of sensory and psychological longing? Is it fair to force me to remain dissatisfied and unfulfilled for the remaining seven days of my life?"

The young woman urged her father and the sage to look at things from her perspective, and when Vashishtha had thought about it thoroughly he concluded that the principles of knowledge and non-attachment—and even the idea of enlightenment itself—cannot be imposed; knowledge must manifest from within. The powerful drive of worldly desires must be acknowledged and transformed. If aspirants are to start smoothly, continue safely, and reach the goal of enlightenment peacefully, they must not fight their natural urges. Thus Vashishtha advised the young woman to get married, enjoy the pleasures she was seeking, and at the same time remain aware of how transitory and superficial they are. Constant awareness of the unsatisfactory nature of worldly pleasures, he explained, together with a natural longing to attain eternal peace and joy within, would help her gain freedom from worldly desires and become established in the real Self.

In seven days Vashishtha witnessed the galaxy's destruction. And the whole experience of leaving the Earth, meditating in empty space, encountering the young woman, and witnessing the destruction of the galaxy led him to reevaluate his concept of peace and how to attain it. He realized that the mind can fill even empty space and create a crowd even in a void. Since he had nothing but the mind to verify what had taken place, he wondered if what he had witnessed had actually happened. His mind's inability to know for certain what was real led him to doubt that the world we live in is real. And from this, Vashishtha formulated the philosophy of reflectionism.

In Sanskrit the philosophy of reflectionism is known as *abhasa vada* or *pratibimba vada*. It maintains that this universe of ours is only a projection of the mind, and that the world has no essence of its own—the mind simply projects its own contents on it and then believes that these projections are real. A strong belief in the validity of worldly objects brings a sense of stability, and the stronger the belief in the world, the longer that world lasts. But the moment the mind sees its own tricks—its projection and its firm belief in the objects it has created—this entire make-believe structure vanishes. In other words, this world is merely a creation of the mind.

This is also true of internal states such as peace and happiness. First, the mind creates a condition of dissatisfaction and then lets itself believe that it is miserable. And once it realizes it is miserable, it cannot be happy until it has overcome this misery. That is how the tricky mind begins its peace pilgrimage. The farther it walks on this journey the more miserable it becomes, until, one day, either someone reminds the mind that it is simply projecting its own contents, or it remembers by itself.

At that point the thinking process goes something like this: "O mind, there is no shrine of peace outside you. Change the direction of your journey and find peace within. In order to turn inward, you must first transcend your own belief system—the belief that someone else will give you salvation, that someone else will make you happy. In order to find peace, O mind, you must first overcome your habit of tricking yourself, of making your own projections and then getting entangled in them. Make yourself simple. Learn to be quiet rather than hyperactive. Do not mistake an object you attain for peace. Rather, understand that peace is a mental state that is always present. It is a state of stillness. Through your own self-created noise you disturb that state, and only you can remove the disturbance."

The complete inner dialogue between Vashishtha and his mind is beautifully narrated by Valmiki in the *Yoga Vashishtha,* a treasure-trove of Vashishtha's spiritual wisdom which Vashishtha shared with Rama, his beloved disciple. Rama was a prince who had come to study with Vashishtha at an early age. Rama returned to his father after completing his formal education at Vashishtha's ashram, but soon thereafter fell into a deep depression. The king, distraught, sought Vashishtha's wise counsel, and Vashishtha advised him to send Rama to visit holy places and learn from the saints and yogis.

After several years of wandering, Rama gained some peace of mind, but he was not fully content. So he returned to live in Vashishtha's ashram once again. By now he was fully prepared for the higher teachings, and on many different occasions student and enlightened sage discussed those issues that every sincere aspirant faces sooner or later. The following dialogue is a sample of an exchange between the master and his disciple.

R a m a : What should I do to unveil the subtle mysteries of life and attain peace and happiness?

V a s h i s h t h a : Mind is the greatest of all mysteries. It stands between you and the highest truth, and it is the cause of both bondage and liberation. Properly trained, mind can help you attain enlightenment; if misguided, it can leave you stranded on the shoals of confusion and bondage. Peace is created by the mind, Rama. So first, make the decision to be content in any circumstance. From that womb, peace is born. It is foolish to expect to achieve peace by retiring into the deep forest or leaving for a distant galaxy. Ultimately you must find peace within yourself.

R a m a : Why does the mind prefer to run in the external world rather than turning inward to find peace?

V a s h i s h t h a : The mind has bound itself tightly to the senses, and driven by sense cravings, it runs to the external world. As long as you do not know how to withdraw the senses from the external world you have almost no choice but to let your mind remain a victim of sense pleasure.

The objects of the senses, however, as well as the pleasure derived from them, are momentary. Soon after experiencing a sensory pleasure, the mind realizes the emptiness of the experience. But not knowing where to find satisfaction, it turns again to the external world. Thus dissatisfaction becomes a way of life. The constant failure to experience joy leads to frustration. Peace is lost, and the inner world becomes chaotic. Inner discontent, frustration, and restlessness then manifest in one's external life, and both the internal and external worlds are full of misery.

R a m a : What is the solution?

V a s h i s h t h a : Non-attachment is the only way to overcome this strife. When aspirants cultivate this attitude, they come to realize that all the objects of the world are transitory and that the value of worldly objects is simply a creation of the mind. Once they realize that they came into the world with nothing and will depart with nothing, they will not be attached to the objects of the world.

R a m a : I know that this is true, but somehow I fail to maintain this knowledge, especially when it comes to interacting with the world.

V a s h i s h t h a : That is because the mind is fully convinced that this world and its objects are real; this is called maya. It is a strong belief in the existence of that which does not exist. To illustrate this point, let me tell you a story.

Once a washerman asked his son to go to the barn and get his donkey, but when the boy tried to fetch the animal, it wouldn't budge. So the boy went to his father and told him what had happened.

"Is the donkey tied up?" the washerman asked.

"No. That's what I don't understand," the son replied.

"Well then, slap him on the rump to get him moving!" the father replied in exasperation.

The son tried this but the donkey still wouldn't move. So the boy went back to his father and said, "Father, he must be sick. Please come and see for yourself."

This time father and son went to the barn together, and the

father also tried to get the donkey to move. To no avail. Then suddenly he understood the problem. Taking the rope, which was attached to the donkey's halter but not attached to the post, he wound it around the post. Then he unwound it and began walking out of the barn. Only then did the donkey follow him.

This, Rama, is the case with those whose minds are convinced of the reality of worldly objects and the bondage they create. But this world is not capable of binding either mind or soul; the mind is in bondage simply because it believes that it is.

R a m a : How can the mind overcome this illusion?

V a s h i s h t h a : First, through constant contemplation on the illusory nature of worldly pleasure the mind must overcome its craving for worldly objects. Second, the mind must recognize its true nature and maintain that awareness constantly.

Forgetting the true nature of the Self is what makes human beings subject to timidity, weakness, fear, and insecurity. And it is this forgetfulness that causes us to keep searching for a haven in the external world. But once we realize our inner Self, we are free from the charms of the world as well as the fear of death. I will tell you another ancient tale to illustrate this point.

Once a lion cub was separated from the pride right after birth. His eyes had not yet opened, and thus he never saw his mother. He was helpless, but after a few days a flock of sheep happened by, so he joined them and was raised with the lambs. As a result, he identified with the sheep and learned to behave like them. He learned to follow others blindly, to be afraid of dogs, and to submit when he was whipped by the shepherd. He grew to full adulthood, but because he constantly saw the sheep that surrounded him, and because his identification with them was complete, he had never noticed how big he was or what sharp, powerful claws he had. He never found out how fast he could run, how high he could jump, how loud he could roar.

One day another lion crept up on the flock and let out a tremendous roar. The flock scattered. The young lion, who was as frightened as the sheep, ran away too. But, in full flight, he happened to see his reflection in a pond, and to his astonishment, it resembled the lion he was running from. He was confused. Why didn't he look like the other sheep? He went back to examine the reflection. At first he was disappointed because he expected to see a sheep, but this quickly turned into curiosity. As an experiment he tried to roar like the lion he had just heard—and found that he could! This filled his mind with delight and wonder. He jumped and roared some more, and relished the realization that he was truly a lion. He never returned to the flock, but joined the pride and lived as the king of the forest.

31

You see, Rama, through our identification we create a self-image, and based on that we create a reality. If this identification is false, we are victims of falsehood. If the identification is correct, then we are fortunate enough to live in the light of truth.

R a m a : I understand, *Gurudeva*. Overcoming the charms and temptations of the world, turning the mind inward, and attaining a true glimpse of oneself is possible through *vairagya* [non-attachment]. But the essence of vairagya is too subtle for me to grasp. Furthermore, while I am trying to practice vairagya, how do I deal with my other weaknesses, which distract me during sadhana?

V a s h i s h t h a : Learn to withdraw your senses and mind systematically before you practice vairagya or commit yourself to any intense practice of contemplation or meditation. This process is called *pratyahara* [sense withdrawal].

In the following discourse Vashishtha teaches Rama how to practice pratyahara.

V a s h i s h t h a : People who search for joy in the external world, Rama, are always disappointed. Desires and cravings begin in the mind, and the mind then motivates the senses to contact objects. That is why trying to control the senses alone will not be effective.

The first step in pratyahara is to convince the mind and senses that it is necessary to withdraw. To do this, you must find out why the mind is running in the external world. Then you will discover that the mind and senses keep busy in the external world or resort to sleep in order to escape from reality, which is painful. But the external search for peace is very tiring, and sooner or later the mind stops to rest. This feels good, and if the mind can be made to see and acknowledge the effect of rest, it will begin to develop a willingness to rest and withdraw the senses.

When we pull in the mind and senses voluntarily with the thread of knowledge, we experience true relaxation. And after the mind experiences the joyful stillness in the body that results from pratyahara, it can be successfully instructed to look within for the true source of happiness.

There are three ways of practicing pratyahara, Rama. The first is to withdraw the senses and mind from the external world, and then to focus them consciously on a chosen object in the realm of the mind. Another way to practice is to see everything in the world as existing within the Atman, the Self. Then there is nothing outside the Atman, so there is no need to withdraw the senses. A third practice is to carry out all your activities as if they were sacred duties. In this way you bring sanctity to even the most mundane aspects of life.

If you cannot control your senses immediately, Rama, do not be discouraged. The process by which the senses move toward their objects is very subtle. It begins with thinking—you become attached to something just by thinking about it. Something becomes attractive because of inner cravings or because of latent impressions from the past that exist in the mind. The *samskaras* and *vasanas* in the mind see something similar to themselves in the external objects and feel joy in this correspondence. The inner experience of full identification is called enjoyment. In that affinity or feeling of sympathy you say "This belongs to me." Attachment follows that thought.

In other words, attachment arises from merely thinking about something. The desire to act is based on that attachment, and if something impedes that action, we become angry. If we find that the impediment cannot be overcome, we become depressed, or, if we feel strong, we might fight the obstruction. That produces anger. From anger arises delusion, and from delusion, loss of memory. With loss of memory, *buddhi* [the power of discrimination] is lost, and it is then impossible to decide anything appropriately. At this point a human being is doomed.

So study yourself, Rama, because only then can you build the foundation you need for withdrawing your senses and mind. Look at the nature of pleasure and pain and determine for yourself what happens when you are attached to the world of names and forms. As a human being, you have the freedom to create your world; controlling the senses is your birthright. Therefore practice pratyahara to conserve your energies, and then concentrate and focus these energies one-pointedly.

Vashishtha then tells Rama about the six qualities of mind— the six prerequisites that students must cultivate before committing themselves to the practice of any spiritual discipline.

V a s h i s h t h a : Now, Rama, I will teach you how to create an environment in which self-transformation can more easily take place. While you are controlling the activities of the senses and withdrawing them from their objects, you must adopt a healthy philosophy of life, one that will create a good environment for your self-transformation. There are six qualities of mind that will help you accomplish this: *shama, dama, titiksha, uparati, samadhana,* and *mumuksha.*

Shama is quietude of mind, tranquility, equanimity, and composure. First, learn to compose yourself. Rather than expecting the external world to conform to your expectations, learn to expect the unexpected. Regard turmoil as normal and take worldly blows in stride. Expecting things to be perfect leads to disappointment. Disappointment and tranquility cannot coexist.

An average person feels happy in response to happy events, and miserable in the face of sad events. Such a one is tossed by the tides of the external world, and for him happiness becomes purely accidental. To attain tranquility you must learn not to be influenced by external circumstances. That is the only way to find the state of stillness within. And once you know how to remain still, you can study both the external and the internal worlds.

Dama is self-restraint, self-control, self-mastery, and control over your senses. The activities of the senses are the first step in the formation of habit patterns. The conscious mind is connected to the senses, and it is through the senses that the conscious mind interacts with the objects of the external world. If the mind is not trained properly, then the senses become its guiding force, and the mind follows them helplessly. This helplessness occurs because the mind gives too much importance to sensory objects and too much authority to the senses. Consequently, they take over.

The senses are like the horses that pull a chariot. The body is the chariot, the mind is the reins, and the intellect is the driver. The soul dwells in the body-mind organism, and if the horses are untrained and not properly connected to the reins, they can destroy both the chariot and the driver. Even if the reins are strong and held tightly in the hands of the driver, wild horses can still create serious problems.

Therefore training the senses is of the utmost importance. It must be based on proper understanding, because if you try to restrain your senses without it, repression and suppression will result. You must be fully convinced of the importance of being happy and healthy, and you must understand that control over your senses maintains that state. Using knowledge as the basis for controlling the senses is discipline, but this discipline must be lovingly accepted by your mind, not imposed on it.

Titiksha is forbearance, tolerance, and endurance at the physical, mental, and verbal levels. Expand your capacity to face every situation and circumstance that life brings. Coping with the world requires endurance and forbearance. Be ready for anything in life, because anything can happen.

The body has enormous capacities—it is simply a matter of unfolding them. Do not allow yourself to become dependent on external objects. It is important to live a comfortable life and to have a regular schedule. But do not let comfort make you lazy, and do not let regularity lapse into rigidity. Maintaining a degree of flexibility is also part of discipline. Learning to endure the discomfort brought about by heat, cold, hunger, thirst, fatigue, and sleepiness is part of the practice of titiksha. Develop the ability to adjust yourself to every situation.

Uparati means desisting from sensual pleasure. There is a difference between craving objects and needing objects. You must make a sincere effort to earn your livelihood. And after you have earned it, enjoy it. But even though you have means and resources, you should be able to withdraw yourself whenever you wish, and you can do this only when you are not involved with the objects you have acquired. If you get involved, if you start analyzing how much time and energy you have put into gaining objects—how hard you worked, how many years it took, and therefore how valuable these objects are—then you create a strong attachment to them. By keeping track of all these details, we bind ourselves with the objects of the world.

If you take your success too seriously, you get entangled in it and fail to use the objects of your success as a means for the next level of achievement—the spiritual. Thus, right from the beginning of your worldly endeavors, desist from the cravings of the senses and maintain an awareness that even though worldly objects provide a degree of comfort, ultimately they are worthless.

Therefore, Rama, work hard, but once the work is done, forget it. Think and feel as though you have done nothing. Cultivate an attitude of forgetfulness. Perform your actions, but when you receive the fruit, take it as a gift from above. This is uparati, and it is the ground on which you practice non-attachment.

Samadhana is putting together, or arranging in proper order. This refers to putting the statements of different teachers and scriptures in their proper context. There are many philosophies, many instructions, and in most cases they appear to be contradictory. For example, it is said that the objects of the world are completely illusory—like objects in a dream, they are totally worthless. But it is also said that even though all the objects in the world evolve from God and are meant for God, you should enjoy them without getting attached to them. If you do not develop the ability to place these statements in their proper context, you will be confused.

Here is another example of samadhana: It is said that the path of karma [action] is as valid as the path of knowledge. Yet it is also said that one cannot attain the highest realization by performing one's actions, because it is through knowledge, not karma, that one gains liberation. Again, without the ability to place these statements in their proper context you will be confused and wonder: "If actions cannot help me attain freedom, no matter how beautifully and skillfully I perform them, then why should I bother performing actions?" Learned teachers resolve this conflict by pointing out that if you do not perform your actions skillfully, they will create obstacles, no matter what spiritual path you are treading. But performing your actions skillfully allows you to live in this world happily while minimizing the obstacles. If you have the ability to put things in the proper context you will understand that the paths of karma and knowledge are complementary.

Mumuksha is the desire for liberation. Without it, spiritual practice is merely art: you'll become an accomplished philosopher who is miserable from carrying the burden of knowledge without the benefit of experience. If you study out of curiosity or for the sake of studying itself, you become a pedant or a logician.

Many people learn so much that they lose their faith. They keep studying and finding contradictions. Because they lack mumuksha, they do not understand the principle of samadhana—how to put things in their proper order. But once you desire liberation, everything falls into place. Everything makes sense, and you become tongue-tied. You understand that all this doesn't make sense to many people, but you will not waste your time explaining it to them because they don't have the strength of desire necessary to understand. That's why the *Upanishads* say, "Those who think it is known to them know nothing at all. And those who do not think it is known to them might know it." Once you know, you cannot express it because it is so subtle.

You can answer the questions that grow out of mere curiosity yourself. If you study the nature of your curiosity and the source from which it grows, you will find the answers. But you will find that there are certain powerful questions that you cannot answer. They don't allow you to sit peacefully, but drag you from one book to another, from one place to another, from one teacher to another. That is the power of mumuksha—the desire for liberation.

The knowledge that Vashishtha imparted to the world is found throughout Vedic, Upanishadic, and Puranic literature, but *Yoga Vashishtha, Vashishtha Samhita,* and the portions of the *Vedas* said to have come through Vashishtha are the main sources of his teaching. *Yoga Vashishtha* is an encyclopedic text in which the great sage teaches the practical aspect of yogic disciplines related to body, breath, and mind. It contains precise techniques of pranayama, concentration, and sense withdrawal, but it also blends yogic practices with the sublime teachings of Vedanta (*jñana* yoga). In the 24,000 verses that constitute this text, Vashishtha raises and resolves issues related to almost every aspect of life. The underlying theme is *vairagya* (non-attachment), but it is fully balanced with *abhyasa* (the actual yogic practices).

The highest level of knowledge imparted by Vashishtha, however, was supposedly contained in another text, called *Vashishtha Samhita,* which no longer exists. References to it are found throughout the spiritual literature of the Himalayas, and it is assumed that it was one of the most authoritative texts of the highest branch of tantra—the *samaya* school of *Sri Vidya*—which maintains the inner essence of the Vedic tradition. Here aspirants learn the pure yogic techniques of going inward and attaining the experience of oneness with Shiva and Shakti. Fragments from this lost text are found in the form of quotations in other texts, but the knowledge Vashishtha imparted in this work is preserved intact only in the oral tradition of the Himalayan masters.

DATTATREYA

Dattatreya's father, Atri, and his mother, Anasuya, were both famous sages, but because of his profound wisdom and yogic achievements Dattatreya himself is viewed not only as a sage but also as an incarnation of God. He is thought to be an incarnation of Brahma and Vishnu, as well as Shiva.

The places where Dattatreya lived (and still lives, some think, in his subtle form) are charged with such spiritual energy that even novice seekers who travel there are affected by it. There are several such places in the hills of Nilachala in eastern India and several more in the Himalayas, but the most famous site is Girinar in Gujarat on the west coast of India.

The ashram of Dattatreya's parents, known as Anasuya, still exists in Chitrakut, nestled in the beautiful Vindhya range of the central Indian mountains. A steep mountain towers over the back of the ashram, and the serene streams of the Mandakini River issue from a nearby cave. There is a pervasive sense of fearlessness and tranquility in the air. Fish leap from the water to take puffed rice from the hands of pilgrims. Monkeys come from the forest, greet visitors, and share their food like old friends. Your intellect may insist that they do it simply to get food, but listen to nature and you will hear a silent voice: "Do not pollute the spirit of the sages with your cold intellectualism."

One day when Dattatreya was still a child the king of a neighboring country came to visit the ashram, and because his parents were away, the boy greeted the guest in the palace. As Dattatreya made arrangements for the visitor's comfort, the king saw an inner joy radiating from the boy's countenance. And realizing that this was a spontaneous expression of the intrinsic beauty of the boy's soul, he was sure that Dattatreya was gifted with great wisdom. Curious to learn how someone so young could be so wise, the king questioned the child, and the following dialogue ensued.

K i n g : You have been studying with your parents?

D a t t a t r e y a : There is much to learn from everyone and everything, not only from my parents.

K i n g : Then you have a teacher? Who is it?

D a t t a t r e y a : I have 24 gurus [spiritual masters].

K i n g : Twenty-four gurus at such a tender age? Who are they?

D a t t a t r e y a : Mother Earth is my first guru. She taught me to hold lovingly in my heart all those who trample me, scratch me, and hurt me, just as she does. She taught me to give them my best, remembering that their acts are normal and natural from their standpoint.

K i n g : Who is your second guru?

D a t t a t r e y a : Water. This force contains life and purity. It cleanses whatever it touches and provides life to whoever drinks it. Water flows unceasingly. If it stops, it becomes stagnant. "Keep moving, keep moving" is the lesson I learned from water.

K i n g : Your third guru?

D a t t a t r e y a : Fire. It burns everything, transforming it into flame. By consuming dead logs, it produces warmth and light. Thus, I learn to absorb everything that life brings and turn it into the flame that enlightens my life. In that light, others can walk safely.

K i n g : Who is your fourth guru, sir?

Dattatreya: The wind is my fourth guru. The wind moves unceasingly, touching flowers and thorns alike, but it never attaches itself to the objects it touches. Like the wind, I learned not to prefer flowers over thorns, or friends over foes. Like the wind, my goal is to provide freshness to all without becoming attached.

King: The fifth guru, sir?

Dattatreya: All-pervading and all-embracing space is my fifth guru. Space has room for the sun, moon, and stars, and yet it remains untouched and unconfined. I, too, must have room for all the diversities of existence and still remain unaffected by what I contain. All visible and invisible objects have their rightful place within me, but they have no power to confine my consciousness.

King: Who is your sixth guru, sir?

Dattatreya: The moon. The moon waxes and wanes, and yet it never loses its essence, totality, or shape. From watching the moon I learned that waxing and waning, rising and falling, pleasure and pain, loss and gain are simply phases of life. While passing through these phases I never lose awareness of my true Self.

King: Who is your seventh guru?

Dattatreya: The sun is my seventh guru. With its bright rays, the sun draws water from everything, transforms it into clouds, and then distributes it without favor as rain. Rain falls on forests, mountains, valleys, deserts, oceans, and cities. Like the sun, I learned how to gather knowledge from all sources, transform that knowledge into practical wisdom, and share it with all without preferring some recipients and excluding others.

King: And your eighth guru?

Dattatreya: My eighth guru is a flock of pigeons. When one fell into a hunter's net and cried in despair, the other pigeons tried to rescue it and got caught, too. From these pigeons I learned that even a positive reaction, if it springs from attachment and emotion, can entangle and ensnare.

King: Your ninth guru, sir?

Dattatreya: My ninth guru is the python who catches

and eats its prey, and then doesn't hunt again for a long time. It taught me that once my need has been met, I must be satisfied and not make myself miserable running after the objects of my desire.

K i n g : Who is your tenth guru?

D a t t a t r e y a : The ocean, which is the abode of the waters. It receives and assimilates water from all the rivers in the world, and yet it never overflows its boundaries. The ocean taught me that no matter what experiences I go through in life, no matter how many kicks and blows I receive, I must maintain my discipline.

K i n g : Who is your eleventh guru, O wise one?

D a t t a t r e y a : The moth is my eleventh guru. Drawn by light, it flies from its dwelling to sacrifice itself in the flame. It taught me that once I see the dawn, I must overcome my fear, soar at full speed, and plunge into the flame of knowledge to be consumed and transformed.

K i n g : The twelfth?

D a t t a t r e y a : My twelfth guru is the bumblebee, who takes only the tiniest drops of nectar from the flowers. And before accepting even that much, it hums and hovers and dances, creating an atmosphere of joy around the blossom. It not only sings the song of cheerfulness, it also gives more to the flowers than it takes: it pollinates the plants and helps them prosper by flying from one to another. I learned from the bumblebee that I should take only a little from nature and that I should do so cheerfully, enriching the source from which I receive sustenance.

K i n g : Your thirteenth guru?

D a t t a t r e y a : My thirteenth guru is the honeybee, who collects more nectar than it needs. It gathers nectar from different sources, swallows it, transforms it into honey, and brings it to the hive. It consumes only a bit of what it gathers, and shares the rest with others. Thus, I should gather wisdom from the teachers of all disciplines and process the knowledge that I gain. I must apply the knowledge that is conducive to my own growth, but I must be ready to share everything I know with others.

K i n g : The fourteenth guru, O wise seeker?

D a t t a t r e y a : Once I saw a wild elephant being trapped. A tame female elephant in season was the bait. Sensing her presence, the wild male emerged from its domain and fell into a pit that had been cleverly concealed with branches and heaps of leaves. Once caught, the wild elephant was tamed to be used by others. This elephant is my fourteenth guru because he taught me to be careful with my passions and desires. Worldly charms arouse our sensory impulses, and while chasing after the sense cravings the mind gets trapped and enslaved, even though it is powerful.

K i n g : Who is your fifteenth guru, sir?

D a t t a t r e y a : The deer, with its keen sense of hearing. It listens intently and is wary of all noises—but it is lured to its doom by the melody of the deer hunter's flute. Like the deer, we keep our ears alert for every bit of news, rumor, and gossip, and are skeptical about much that we hear. What I learned from the deer is that we become spellbound by certain words which—due to our desires, attachments, cravings, and *vasanas* [subtle impressions from the past]—we delight to hear. This tendency creates misery for ourselves and others.

K i n g : And who is your sixteenth guru?

D a t t a t r e y a : The fish who swallows a baited hook and is caught by the fisherman. This world is like bait. As long as I remember the fish, I remain free of the hook.

K i n g : Who is your seventeenth guru?

D a t t a t r e y a : A prostitute. She knows that she doesn't love her customers, nor do they love her. She waits for them, and when they come she enacts the drama of love, but she isn't satisfied with the artificial love she gives and receives, nor with the payment she is given. Through her I realized that all humans are like prostitutes, and the world, like the customers, is enjoying us. The payment is always inadequate and we feel dissatisfied. Thus I determined not to live like a prostitute. Instead, I will live with dignity and self-respect. I will not expect this world to give me either material or

43

internal satisfaction. I will find satisfaction myself by going within.

K i n g : Who is your eighteenth guru?

D a t t a t r e y a : My eighteenth guru is the little bird who was flying with a worm in its beak. Larger birds flew after him and began to peck him. They stopped only when the little bird dropped the worm. Thus I learned that the secret of survival lies in renunciation, not in possession.

K i n g : Who is your nineteenth guru, sir?

D a t t a t r e y a : My nineteenth guru is the baby that cries when it is hungry and stops when it suckles at its mother's breast. When the baby is full, it stops feeding, and nothing its mother does can induce it to take more milk. I learned from this baby to demand only what I really need. When it is provided, I must take only what I require and then turn my face away.

K i n g : And your twentieth guru?

D a t t a t r e y a : A young woman whom I met when I was begging for alms. She told me to wait while she prepared a meal. Her bracelets jangled as she cooked, so she removed one. But the noise continued, so she took them all off one by one until only one remained. Then there was silence. Thus I learned that wherever there is a crowd, there is noise, disagreement, and dissension. Peace can be expected only in solitude.

K i n g : And your twenty-first guru?

D a t t a t r e y a : A snake who makes no hole for itself, but rests in holes other creatures have abandoned, or curls up in the hollow of a tree for a while, and then moves on. From this snake I learned to adjust myself to my environment and enjoy the resources of nature without encumbering myself with a permanent home. Creatures in nature move constantly, continually abandoning their previous dwellings. Therefore, while floating along the current of nature, I find plenty of places to rest. Once I am rested, I move on.

K i n g : And your twenty-second guru?

D a t t a t r e y a : My twenty-second guru is the arrow-maker who was so absorbed in shaping his arrowheads that the king and his entire army passed nearby without attracting his attention. Thus I learned to be absorbed in the task at hand, no matter how big or small. The more one-pointed my focus, the greater my absorption, and the greater my absorption, the more subtle my awareness. The goal is subtle; it can be grasped only by subtle awareness.

K i n g : Your twenty-third guru?

D a t t a t r e y a : My twenty-third guru is the little spider who built itself a nice cozy web. When a larger spider chased it, it rushed to take refuge in its web. But it ran so fast that it got entangled and was swallowed by the bigger spider. Thus I learned that we create webs for ourselves by trying to build a safe haven, and as we race along the threads of these webs, we become entangled and are consumed. There is no safety to be found in the complicated webs of our actions.

K i n g : And who is your twenty-fourth guru?

D a t t a t r e y a : My twenty-fourth guru is the worm who was caught by a songbird and placed in its nest. As the bird began to sing, the worm became so absorbed in the song that it lost all awareness of its peril. Watching this little creature become absorbed in a song in the face of death reminded me that I, too, must develop the art of listening so that I may become absorbed in the eternal sound, *nada*, that is always within me.

Listening to Dattatreya, the king realized that the wisdom of this young sage flowed from his determination to keep the goal of life firmly fixed in his awareness as well as from his ability to discover the lessons of life everywhere he turned.

Dattatreya's teachings are preserved in the vast literature of the *Puranas* and in the *Datta Samhita, Avadhuta Gita, Dattatreya Upanishad,* and *Advadhuta Upanishad.* This story is from the *Srimad Bhagavatam.* Many of these works are available in English.

PARASHURAMA

In his early childhood Parashurama was keenly interested in the martial arts and the science of archery, but completely indifferent to philosophy and spiritual practice. Although his father, Jamadagni, and his mother, Renuka, were both great sages, and even though he was kindhearted in general, Parashurama had no mercy for those who violated the principles he held sacred. Toward them he showed no forgiveness. He loved his father, his mother, and his guru more than he loved himself or God, and he would not tolerate even the least slight to them. But outside of that, he was infinitely forgiving, merciful, and compassionate toward others.

His learned father, Jamadagni, was the chancellor of a large education center as well as a famous teacher, and he allowed his son to grow according to his natural inclinations. In those days the martial arts and the science of weaponry far surpassed anything that we know today—weapons were wielded mainly through the power of thought or involved the use of sound waves (mantras)—and Jamadagni made arrangements for his son to study with masters of these disciplines.

Parashurama was a brilliant pupil. He soon mastered all the

weapons of warfare that had ever been invented as well as those (as legend has it) which were yet to be invented. And he also mastered all of the martial arts. By the time he completed his training, his skill as a warrior was unsurpassed.

In keeping with the disciplines of the martial arts, Parashurama decided to remain celibate for his entire life and dedicate himself to the service of his parents and teachers. His plan was to live in peace—but this was not to be. As fate would have it, his father incurred the enmity of a powerful king, who visited Jamadagni's ashram one day, accompanied by an enormous retinue. To the king's surprise, he was greeted with royal honors. And curious to know how the sage could afford such a splendid reception, he inquired about the source of the ashram's wealth. Parashurama's father replied simply that his cows were his only wealth. The king pressed him further, and he finally explained that one of the cows—Kamadhenu—was special. It was the only one of its kind in the world.

This aroused the king's curiosity even more. He asked to see the cow. And when Jamadagni had it brought before them, the king demanded that it be given to him. The sage objected. "It does not befit you to make such demands," he said. "This cow enables me to support myself and to provide for the education of all the students who live in the ashram. You are a king. Your actions should set an example for others. If someone does not want to give away his possessions, he should not be forced to do so. This is a basic law."

Furious, the king determined to possess the cow, but he knew that if he used force against someone as beloved as Jamadagni his people would rise up, and the ensuing revolt might well cost him his kingdom. So he swallowed his anger and decided to bide his time.

When Parashurama learned what had happened, he was enraged, as he always was in the face of an insult or threat to those he loved. But the king had made no move to take the cow or harm his father, so the boy was persuaded to leave him alone. Months passed uneventfully. Then one afternoon, when Parashurama had gone to the forest to gather fruits and nuts, the king stole into the ashram where Jamadagni was sitting alone, deeply immersed in meditation. Seizing his opportunity, the king cut off the sage's head and fled with the coveted cow.

Parashurama returned to find his mother weeping beside his father's corpse. Consumed by rage, he vowed to his mother: "The land that has absorbed your tears will be drenched with the blood of those who are intoxicated with the liquor of power."

Single-handedly Parashurama obliterated the king and his entire army, and then went on to kill the king's relatives and thousands of his subjects. Only those who fled the country survived. The young man's fury did not cool until he could no longer find any members or supporters of that royal clan.

Then, almost immediately, Parashurama was filled with remorse. He should have limited his vengeance to those who were responsible for his father's murder, he realized, and so he went to his guru, Kashyapa, for advice. He was told to devote his time and energy to spiritual practice.

Parashurama immersed himself in those pursuits, and several years passed peacefully. Then, by chance, he heard that some of the king's clan had fled during the war and were now multiplying and prospering in another region. The memory of his father's murder flooded back, and in a surge of uncontrollable anger he conquered the land to which these people had fled and killed everyone who had any connection with them. That done, he was again filled with remorse and racked with self-condemnation. He returned to his spiritual practice, vowing never to kill again. But soon word of a pocket of survivors reached him once more, and without thinking he slaughtered them all. This happened twenty-one times, until at last, burdened with guilt and filled with self-loathing, Parashurama went to his teacher and pleaded for help. Kashyapa advised him to take refuge in the great sage Dattatreya, who lived in the hills of Gandhamadana.

Drowning in waves of frustration, dejection, and a sense of

hopelessness, Parashurama set out to find Dattatreya. As he drew near to Dattatreya's dwelling place, he felt as though the invisible hands of nature were removing the burden he had been carrying for years. Never since his father's murder had he seen such beauty in the earth, tasted such purity in the water, or smelled such freshness in the air. It seemed as though even the plants and animals were enjoying boundless freedom and peace.

Parashurama found Dattatreya sitting on a boulder surrounded by dogs, jackals, snakes, and birds, the aura around his face brighter than the sun and more cooling than the moon. At this first glimpse Parashurama was pulled toward the great master like an iron filing to a magnet. He was released from the limits of time and space, and the next moment he found himself at the sage's feet. Parashurama began to tell the sage about his misery, but Dattatreya quickly interrupted him, saying, "There is no need of recounting your past deeds, O son of Jamadagni and Renuka! The past is dead and you are reborn in the present."

With this, Dattatreya placed his hands on Parashurama's head, and the boy was transformed instantly. Grief vanished. The violent warrior became a spiritual aspirant. The conqueror of enemies turned into a seeker of divine grace.

In the company of Dattatreya, Parashurama found solace of mind, and as he lived and served his master he learned the highest wisdom of *Sri Vidya* (the mystical scientific path leading to the highest beauty and bliss). Then, after receiving formal initiation in this discipline, he was instructed to complete a twelve-year practice in solitude. So Parashurama moved to the Nilachala Hills in the land of Assam, where he built his hut and underwent twelve years of sadhana.

The Nilachala Hills are among the most beautiful places in eastern India. Heavy rain and the absence of efficient transportation prevent casual pilgrims and spiritual seekers from reaching them, and no trace of Parashurama's cottage or any other man-made structure remains today. But the spring from which he used to get his water bears his name and is still flowing. According to legend, Parashurama himself created the pool formed by this spring, and today it is known locally as *Parashurama Kunda,* the pool of Parashurama. Spiritual aspirants and adepts find delight in sipping its water.

When Parashurama completed his practice he returned to his master for further guidance. During his absence he had formulated many profound questions, such as: What is the cause of life and life's experiences? Where does life come from and where does it rest after it vanishes? Everything is in constant flux; human behavior is like one blind person attempting to follow another—does anyone ever get what they really want? And if the desired result is truly achieved, then why do people aspire for more? Parashurama approached his master with these questions, and a series of dialogues ensued. They can be found in the *Jñanakhanda* of *Tripura Rahasya,* of which there are several versions in English. What follows is a few of these dialogues in shortened form.

P a r a s h u r a m a : Master, it seems that whatever is achieved through action is a burden and that the fruits even of good actions are of little value. The absence of happiness is painful, but happiness is transitory. After pleasure ends, a person experiences even greater pain. Spiritual practice seems no different. The end result of all the concentrations and visualizations is not clear.

D a t t a t r e y a : My son, you have now attained true *buddhi* [discriminating knowledge]. You are a rare and fortunate seeker. He who attains such inspired thought is like a drowning man who catches hold of a boat. Worldly people run after tantalizing objects and miss the highest goal of life: Self-realization.

Discrimination is the first rung on the ladder to this highest goal. The ignorant remain caught in the net of confused thinking, and without clarity of mind they cannot decide what is helpful and what is not.

P a r a s h u r a m a : Sir, many people seem wise on the surface but are ignorant inside. Please tell me how to know which is which.

Dattatreya: Purify and sharpen your intellect and let your discrimination, along with the voice of your heart, help you recognize the wise. Decide whether or not having faith in a particular person will lead you to the highest goal. Neither those who involve themselves completely in dry polemics nor those who do not reason at all can be successful in attaining the goal. But one who employs the force of logic and reasoning in light of the wisdom presented in genuine scriptures attains the highest truth.

Parashurama: There are innumerable scriptures, and in many cases they contradict one another. Teachers and commentators differ even about a single scripture. In addition, one's own intellectual convictions vary with time. What should a seeker accept or reject?

Dattatreya: Purify your mind and make it one-pointed so that you can understand the apparent contradictions in various scriptures as well as in the teachings of the sages. Do not allow anyone's teachings or doctrines to confuse you. Select gems of truth from every possible source and integrate them into your personal philosophy of life. Disregard information that diverts your focus.

You can do this when you know how to balance reason and faith. First, abandon polemics and form the habit of relying on constructive reasoning. This will remove your doubts and convince you that the spiritual practice you have undertaken is genuine and fruitful. Then faith will unfold naturally in your heart, and thereafter faith and constructive reasoning will support and guide each other.

This kind of thoughtful consideration, enriched with faith and constructive reasoning, is called *vichara* [discrimination]. It comes through the grace of the divine force, and it is the strongest motivating factor in sadhana. Through discrimination aspirants will certainly find their path, and through practice seekers can tread that path and attain the highest goal.

Parashurama: Sir, you have said at various times that discrimination is the first rung on the ladder to the highest attainment, and that it comes through the grace of the divine force. You have also said that grace is received through meditation, that an aspirant is committed to meditation only if he or she is interested, and that interest develops after hearing about the glory and importance of meditation and its result. And you have said that above all else, the entire process depends on the company of the wise. Would you please elaborate?

D a t t a t r e y a : The company of the wise is the major way to liberation. Here is a story that illustrates my point:

Long ago there was a prince named Hemachuda, who married Hemalekha, the daughter of a sage. He was not aware that she herself was a sage until he discovered, to his dismay, that this beautiful young woman was not interested in worldly pleasures.

When he asked her why, she explained, "The objects that are sources of pleasure cannot be enjoyed forever. No one can have everything he or she desires, and one who gets only a few of those things is not satisfied. In most cases, pleasure is contaminated by suffering. Further, the concept of pleasure is based on one's way of thinking about worldly objects. The concept of beauty too is merely the projection of the mind.

"Let us take the example of a beautiful woman. The woman is outside the man who perceives her, but the perceiver brings her image inside and evaluates her beauty. If he decides that she meets his standard of loveliness, he projects his conception of beauty onto her. And as he thinks about the attractiveness he has projected onto her, this idea is reinforced. Consequently there arises a desire to enjoy her as an object, and as his senses and mind become excited, he begins to experience pleasure. The cause of that excitement is the sense of beauty in his mind. Children who have not yet developed this sense, and yogis who have conquered it, are not aroused even though they see the same woman."

The wise princess elaborated further on the ultimate worthlessness of worldly objects and the painful nature of sensual pleasure, and she was so persuasive that the prince too lost his interest

53

in them. But because his mind had been occupied by worldly objects all of his life, his newfound dispassion left him in a quandary: he could neither completely renounce the material world nor wholeheartedly embrace it. He continued to accept the pleasurable objects that were presented to him because he was still under the influence of subtle cravings, but his enjoyment was undermined by self-condemnation and guilt. Out of habit and hidden desires he was attracted to sense objects, but at the same time, remembering his wife's words, he was repelled. He was constantly upset. He felt as if his entire fortune had been stolen, and he became gloomy and despondent.

The learned princess realized that her husband had the potential for spiritual growth—otherwise dispassion toward worldly objects and a desire for liberation would not have unfolded in him. So she began to lead him on the spiritual path. The first step was to explain that an untrained mind is the root cause of all miseries. "Mind is like a monkey jumping incessantly," she told him. "In order to comprehend the truth, it is necessary to control its modifications and make it one-pointed, sharp, and inward. Thoughtful consideration enriched with faith and constructive reasoning is *vichara*. Try to understand the supreme goal with its help. Then make a sincere effort to achieve that goal. If you become skeptical because you do not seem to be making progress, you become your own enemy. But if you make an effort with full confidence, faith, and courage, you can never fail."

The prince replied, "How does this follow the law of karma? I know that pain and pleasure, loss and gain, and success and failure are results of our previous karmas and that our present life is governed by our past deeds. That is an eternal law. But sometimes it seems as if God interferes with this law, helping some cross the river of pains and miseries while letting others reap the fruits of their karmas."

The princess explained that the law of karma is established by the supreme Lord and applies only to those who are not fully surrendered to the divine force.

"Law and order are created by Him* and maintained by Him. Without His will, there is no way to violate order and law," she said. "Purifying one's mindfield, paying off karmic debts, penetrating the vast domain of maya, and ultimately experiencing the highest truth is a long process. In this odyssey there are numberless chances to slip from the path and take detours. But if aspirants walk in the grace of God and surrender the fruits of every moment, they realize the sublime glory of the supreme truth easily and quickly.

"To self-centered aspirants She grants the fruits of worship and devotion only after their previous karmas are exhausted. But She immediately grants the highest reward of Self-realization to truly selfless devotees. She does not wait for such aspirants' previous karmas to be exhausted. Because She is an embodiment of infinite compassion, She repeals the law of karma and speedily guides seekers to the highest Self. And after attaining it, their karmic debts are paid. After that, if directed by the supreme divine force, Self-realized aspirants may come back to work in the world and honor the law of karma voluntarily."

The princess went on to describe the nature of the immanent and transcendent forms of God. Inspired by her wisdom, the prince studied with learned masters and gained a clear, intellectual understanding of the truth. With the passage of time he was initiated by his wife and committed himself to the practice of meditation with complete faith and determination.

As a result of his sincere practice the prince gradually received the illuminating grace that helped his outward-oriented mind turn inward. Now he understood the meaning of inner joy, and compared to that, he found worldly pleasures tasteless. But at this stage of his spiritual practice he was unable to live in the inner and outer worlds simultaneously. Nor was he able to find the connection between the spiritual and the external worlds.

*In order to convey the idea that the supreme truth or God is neither male nor female nor neuter, the original text uses the terms "Him," "Her," and "It" interchangeably.

One day Hemachuda asked his wife to elaborate on the nature of our own true Self. To his disappointment, she simply said, "Whatever you feel to be yours is without any doubt different from you. So go into solitude, learn to discriminate, and whatever you find to be related to you, distinguish it from your Self and thus realize your true Self. For example, I am your wife; this automatically implies that I am not you. Renounce everything that is yours. The part of you that cannot be renounced is the Self. That you are."

The prince went into seclusion, sat down, and began to think one-pointedly. "Who am I?" he pondered. "This body is not the Self, because it is born and it changes every day. And there are times when I do not experience my body but still remain aware of my existence. Therefore I cannot be my body. By the same token, I cannot be my prana, senses, mind, or intellect. But even though I do not know who I am and what I am, I feel that I am. I can know things through my mind, but how can I know myself? Let me control all my thought constructs. Then I might experience my pure Self."

Having made this resolution, the prince removed all objects from his mindfield with the skill he had developed in his meditation practice. He was suddenly plunged into great darkness. Exhilarated, he was sure this was his Self. But curious to know if there was anything beyond this darkness, he controlled his mind, transcended the darkness, and experienced a flash of infinite light. Then the light vanished. "Am I seeing the Self in different forms?" he wondered. "Let me control my mind again and see what is beyond."

This time he slipped into a deep sleep that gradually shifted to the dream state. When he returned to normal awareness he asked himself, "Was all of this a dream? Now I am confused. Were the light and darkness also phases of a dream? What a tricky mind. Let me try once more."

This time the prince crossed the sleeping state and was absorbed in a state of blissful awareness. But eventually his mind slipped back to the ordinary waking state. Then he wondered, "Was this bliss a mere dream, or the experience of truth? I've never experienced such a profound state of peace. There is no joy like it, but I cannot explain it. I was not unconscious, because I still remember it clearly. I know that I have experienced it, but it is still a mystery."

The prince returned to his wife, told her of his experiences, and asked if what he had experienced was the Self or something else. The princess replied, "My lord, the effort you made to control the modifications of your mind was very helpful. Enlightened masters consider this to be the main means of Self-realization. The Self, however, cannot be attained; only knowledge of the Self can be attained. You can acquire only what you do not already have. Consider this example: An object is shrouded in darkness. When the darkness is removed by the light of a lamp, that object is revealed. Turning the light on to remove the darkness does not create the object. That is also the case with the Self.

"Suppose a man hides a piece of gold and then forgets where he hid it. When he stops thinking about other things and concentrates only on the gold, he will find it. He is able to concentrate on the gold because he already knows what it looks like.

"In the case of the Self, however, the search is more frustrating because people have completely forgotten that it is their own true nature. That is why they believe they have seen the Self after they have removed some of their thought constructs. An unfamiliar image suddenly arises, and they think 'This is Atman.' That is why they must get some concept of the Self through the revealed scriptures or from the enlightened sages. By so doing they won't mistake the projection of their own mind for the Self while they are in meditation. Enrich your understanding of the Self through self-study, discrimination, and contemplation. For direct realization, however, keep practicing."

So the prince undertook another intense spiritual practice and was finally established in the blissful state. The princess saw that her husband was no longer driven outward by his senses and mind, but drawn inward, and for some time she did not disturb him. Then one day, as she entered the room, the prince opened his eyes, but closed them again to reenter that peaceful state. His wife caught his hands and asked, "What do you gain or lose by opening and closing your eyes? Do you not want to share your inner experiences?"

The prince replied, "For the first time in my life I am at peace. All my life I have run after worldly pleasures, but found no peace. Please be kind to me: leave me alone. Why, after realizing this state, are you still entangled in the world? Why don't you stay in this state forever? Why dissipate yourself in the external world?"

The wise princess answered with a smile, "My love, you still have not realized that supreme state of the Self. What you think you understand is like no understanding at all. The highest awareness can never be affected by opening or closing your eyes. It is not attained by action or inaction, by going somewhere or staying at home. How can it be supreme if it is attained by closing your eyes and lost by opening them?

"Unless the millions of knots of delusion are loosened, supreme bliss cannot be reached. Failing to recognize the Self or seeing a difference between the individual soul and God are some of these knots. Untie them. Transcend the duality of wanting and not wanting, liking and disliking, and finally, let that supreme awareness permeate your waking, dreaming, and deep sleep. There must be no wall between any of the aspects of life."

Deflated, the prince continued his spiritual practice. Gradually he attained maturity in his realization and became firm in that consummate state. And after that he lived as a *jivanmukta* (a soul liberated in this lifetime) while enjoying worldly objects, ruling his subjects, amassing wealth, and administering the kingdom.

Thus Dattatreya demonstrated to Parashurama that the company of the sages is the first step in sadhana and remains the guiding force throughout. Those who aspire to the ultimate should seek the fellowship of saints. The rest follows naturally and effortlessly.

Parashurama: *Gurudeva,* in our previous discussion you explained that there is only one reality: pure consciousness; the objective world, including the mind itself, is mere imagination. And while you were explaining this to me, logically it seemed to be correct. Nevertheless, I do not understand why this universe appears to be real. Intellectually I know that the perceptual world is unreal—but still I experience it as being real. And even though many wise people believe it to be unreal, it does in fact exist. Kindly tell me why this universe appears to be real so that my confusion will be removed.

D a t t a t r e y a : The cause of this error is ignorance. Everyone has tightly embraced ignorance with their heart and mind. It is through identification with form that this body is perceived as Atman. And it is through identification with form that this universe appears to be real. The world appears to a person the way he or she believes it to be. Yogis, through the practice of concentration and meditation, experience oneness with their object of concentration. Let me tell you a wonderful story to illustrate my point:

Long, long ago there lived a powerful king who decided to perform *ashvamedha,* the horse sacrifice. According to the rules, one of the king's magnificent horses, closely guarded by the king's army, was set free and allowed to roam wherever it wanted. If it entered a neighboring ruler's territory, that ruler must either pay tribute to the king or try to capture the horse.

The king's army easily conquered all challengers until it came upon the secluded hermitage of a great sage. He was in samadhi when they arrived and thus was not aware that the arrogant soldiers were desecrating the place with their rudeness and contempt. His son, however, was incensed, and challenging them all to battle, he conquered the entire army through his own yogic powers. The few warriors who managed to escape then saw the young yogi lead horse and captives directly into a hillside and walk through the solid rock as if it were air.

The king, astonished at this news, sent his brother, Mahasena, to ask the sage to order his son to release the captives. The sage agreed, and soon the horse as well as the captive soldiers appeared to materialize out of solid rock. Mahasena sent them all back to his brother, but Mahasena stayed behind and humbly asked the sage to explain how the horse and the soldiers could live inside a hill.

The sage replied that his son had always wanted to be a king. "So I instructed him in some specific practices by which he attained the highest yogic power," he said. "Through his *sankalpa shakti,* the power of determination, he created a universe inside this hill, and in that universe he rules the Earth."

Mahasena was eager to visit this universe, so the young man, using his yogic power, pulled Mahasena's subtle body out of his physical body and left the physical body in a pit covered with leaves. Then he and his guest entered the solid rock. Jolted by this separation from his physical body, Mahasena's subtle body lost consciousness, and the young yogi, through his power of determination, united Mahasena's subtle body with a gross body that he materialized inside the hill world.

When Mahasena regained consciousness the young yogi was transporting him across a vast abyss. Above, below, and all around, Mahasena saw infinite, bewildering space. He saw remote planets in a pitch-black sky. He saw the sun, the moon, and the entire galaxy, which seemed to shine like reflections of paradise.

Finally they landed in the Himalayan peaks, where the young yogi was emperor and ruled the Earth. They spent the day touring his kingdom, and Mahasena was amazed at this great manifestation of yogic power. Then they returned to the outside world.

When they arrived they emerged from the hill as casually as they had entered it. The yogi rendered Mahasena's subtle body unconscious, drew it out of the body he had materialized for him, and united it with Mahasena's original physical body. When he regained consciousness, Mahasena was surprised to see that the world around him was greatly altered, and said, "O great sage, what is this new world you are showing me now?"

The yogi replied, "This is the same country that you left. Several thousand years have passed here, though we spent only a day in the world inside the hill. Here the customs, languages, and land formations have all gone through tremendous change. My father is still in samadhi, but in your brother's genealogy many generations have come and gone. There is a huge forest full of wild animals where your capital city once was."

Mahasena collapsed in grief for the loss of his wife, sons, brother, and nephew, but the yogi said, "Have patience. Is it necessary to grieve for your departed relatives? Who are the dead for whom you weep? Are you mourning the departed souls, or the dead bodies?"

Mahasena then bowed at the young yogi's feet and said, "Sir, I am your disciple. Please help me overcome this grief."

The yogi replied, "People who are deluded by the power of maya do not realize their essential nature, and grieve uselessly. But after realizing the Atman they overcome sorrow, just as dreamers overcome their dream identity and concerns. After dreamers awaken from a nightmare, they laugh at themselves for having been anxious. Likewise, those who have realized their true Self and crossed the domain of illusion laugh at people like you who wail piteously over imagined losses."

"But comparing the experience of the waking state with dreams does not seem to be appropriate here," Mahasena objected. "The objects created in a dream simply appear and do not serve any purpose. But the objects of the waking state are real and useful. They are tangible, used by all, and they remain the same throughout the ages."

The yogi replied, "The objects of the waking and dreaming states are alike. A dream tree serves a purpose in the dream—many travelers rest in its shade and eat its fruit. But just as the dream objects disappear when you wake up, so do the things you experience during the waking state disappear when you fall asleep. And like the objects in dreams, all worldly objects are constantly changing. Nothing is stable. The reality of the external world is maintained by your thoughts. If someone thinks this universe is unreal, then for that person it is unreal.

"The world you just saw is such an example. This whole hill is only one mile around, but within it is an entire universe. Was that world a waking reality or was it a dream? Was it real or unreal? One day in that universe is experienced as several thousand years here. Now decide which universe is real. They are like two different dreams—you cannot explain one in terms of the other. You also cannot say that one is real and the other is unreal or that both are real.

"The obvious conclusion is that the whole universe is the projection of one's own mind. Without this, it would disappear in an instant. So do not grieve. Consider this world to be a dream. Atman, the pure Self, is the canvas on which this universe is painted. Atman is the mirror, and the universe is reflected in that mirror."

Mahasena answered with folded hands, "Sir, through your grace I am free from grief. But there is something I still do not understand. You said that all this happens through thought. But no matter how often I think about something, it doesn't necessarily materialize. Because your willful determination is perfect, you could materialize a whole universe inside a hill. But to me this external world and the world inside the hill coexist. Why then are there differences in time and space between these two worlds?"

The yogi replied, "*Sankalpa shakti*, willful determination, is twofold: perfect and imperfect. If willful determination is untouched by doubt it is said to be perfect. And the absence of doubt is the ability to hold one thought in the mind to the exclusion of all others. This external world is projected through the willful thinking of the Creator, and because it is such an intense affirmation, people believe that the universe is real. On the other hand, you are not fully convinced of your own power of will, determination, and projection, and therefore your lack of self-confidence creates an obstacle to your materializing an object through sheer will.

"Perfection in willful thinking can be attained through gems, herbs, yoga, austerities, mantras, and grace. But whatever the means, when you exercise your power of determination you must become so absorbed in it that you are not aware of the fact that you are doing it. Maintain this state until the intended result appears. For the average person, the power of thinking and determination is tainted by doubts and the fear of not being successful. The power of determination is veiled by maya. But when that veil is lifted, you will realize its perfection.

"The fact that a thing exists—whether large or small, anywhere or at any time—depends on one's will. I projected only one day in the world I created, but in your universe the Creator imagined several thousand years. That is why you experience a discrepancy. In a hill one mile around, I visualized infinity; therefore you experienced an endless expanse when you were within it.

"Thus you can see that every experience is both true and untrue. If in your determination you first imagine a one-mile-wide expanse and pair it with one moment of time, and then imagine infinite time and space, both will appear to you as you have imagined. That is the secret behind the relativity of time and space."

P a r a s h u r a m a : Sir, if this entire mess of seeming and not seeming, knowing and not knowing, bondage and liberation is ultimately a game of the mind, and if the way we think—or, let us say, the way we are determined to think—creates the reality behind our experiences, then what is the mind anyway? How is it related to pure consciousness, the Self? Was the mind confused from the very beginning, or did the confusion begin somewhere later? Why is one person's mind so clear, positive, and naturally turned inward, while another's is not?

D a t t a t r e y a : These are the most practical questions you have asked. And from a practical standpoint, unveiling the mystery of the mind is more important than attaining knowledge of the Self, for the Self cannot be realized if the mind is not properly understood. In other words, a properly trained and purified mind is the means for Self-realization, while a dissipated and confused mind is the source of misery. So let me explain the relationship between the mind and the Self or pure consciousness. Ultimately pure consciousness alone exists, but for the sake of our study I propose that mind and consciousness be seen as existing side by side.

Pure consciousness is like an ever-illuminated, self-shining gem that is kept in the safe of the mind. The safe has been sealed for a long time, and because of ignorance and carelessness a thick layer of dust has covered it. The safe is made of a transparent crystal through which the self-shining gem can radiate, illuminating the safe as well as the area around it. But the dust is so thick that it is almost impossible to see the gem. In order to find and enjoy it, the aspirant must begin to clean off the dust. So first clean the safe of the mind, and then you will see that the key is inside, next to the gem. This is a paradox.

Before you can get your key you must be aware of its shape and size, and understand its proper use. For that you need the help of those who have already opened their safes. Such great ones are called realized masters. In their company you have an opportunity to look at your key, at least from the outside of the safe, and by so doing you can begin to understand your mind. You can also observe how easily these masters unlock and lock the safe: how they dwell in two worlds simultaneously—the external and the internal. This will make you acquainted with the map for your own inner odyssey to reach the gem. Later you will have to make the journey by yourself.

No matter how securely the gem of pure consciousness has been locked away, and no matter how thick the veil of impurities, the brilliance of pure consciousness still flashes forth from time to time. That is why people long for Self-realization. Without exception, everyone wants to attain peace and happiness, and therefore the safe of the mind is relatively transparent in places and the gem of pure consciousness is never completely obscured. The Self, the gem, can be attained by removing all of the dust—the impurities in the mind—thus unveiling the gem through your willful determination. And through this process you become identical with the gem. Once the covering dust is removed and the safe of the mind unlocked, you are aware of nothing but the gem itself, and the interior of the mind is ever illumined with the light of pure consciousness.

Parashurama: What are these impurities in the mind, and how are they created?

Dattatreya: There are numberless impurities, but they can be put into three major categories: skepticism, karmic impurity, and a false sense of duty.

Skepticism means improper thinking, lack of faith, not believing what is said in the scriptures and by the saints, or not believing in any higher truth. This is improper, confused thinking, and it is associated with those who know little but think they know a lot.

Such is the case with many philosophers and learned scholars who know the truth intellectually but have not experienced it through spiritual practice. There are many reasons for this, but ego and skepticism are the greatest ones. They may think, "I have studied all the literature of yoga, tantra, Vedanta, and so on. I have even done a comparative study of the various systems of philosophy. I understand all the different viewpoints, and I know more than all the great masters. And since their opinions differ from one another, it indicates that they did not know the truth or knew it only partially. So why should I bother to experience any of these philosophies? I have already drawn my own conclusions."

My son, such people carry the burden of knowledge without any experience, just as a camel carries a huge load of salt, not knowing its taste. And lacking experience, such scholars fight with other scholars, making everyone's life miserable. This type of thinking is confused, and it is a great impediment in spiritual practice. It is caused by mistrusting or contradicting genuine scriptures, and its effect is to create a fresh coating of impurity on the mind. This leads these thinkers further away from Self-realization.

In order to wash off this kind of impurity, sincere seekers must allow the light of the genuine scriptures to penetrate their mind, and they must cultivate faith in the teachings of the selfless, compassionate, enlightened masters. They must recognize that disregarding these masters is an error, and they should have an internal dialogue to convince their mind to follow the guidelines set forth by these masters.

Karmic impurity is the result of every single action we perform, whether mental, verbal, or physical. The subtle impressions of our actions, known as *samskaras,* are stored in the mind, and each time we perform an action we create a little mark in the mindfield. In our numberless lifetimes we have created many such traces. They pollute the transparency of the mind, and as a result the mind becomes dull and loses its spontaneous capacity to comprehend the truth about reality. Karmic impurities also determine the particular species into which we are born and the length of time we spend in it. Our inner tendencies, inclinations, and attitudes are largely governed by these impurities. They tend to counteract the power of determination.

The scriptures describe several means for removing karmic impurities. The fewer there are the clearer a person's mind will be—but without God's grace nothing works efficiently, because any method of purification is actually undertaken by the mind. If it is clouded, then one will not benefit much. Even so, sincere aspirants must not be lazy; they should continue with the technique they have been taught. Through meditation, selfless service, and ultimately God's grace, they will attain the goal. It may be in this lifetime or in a future lifetime, depending on how many of the impurities have been cleared away.

A false sense of duty is the third type of impurity, and this is the most difficult of all to remove because there is no end to worldly duties and obligations. The aspirant must learn to decide which are the most important and take care of those first.

Those who are not awakened to spiritual awareness are driven by their urges and by nature. They remain involved in the world because they do not know life's other dimensions. By the time they complete one project the next is already waiting. But Self-realization is the highest goal of life, and compared to this, all worldly duties are secondary. If this fact is not firmly fixed in the mind there is no way to attain freedom from worldly obligations.

But without spiritual awareness, turning away from the world is a source of misery, and to disregard worldly obligations without having a higher purpose kills your conscience. Therefore, instead of working directly to wash off a false sense of duty, cultivate dispassion and non-attachment, and through constant contemplation let the longing for liberation grow into a burning desire. Only then will you be able to determine whether you should take care of your worldly obligations or renounce them. You attain freedom by conquering your desires, not by running away from your duties. Non-attachment can be cultivated by observing the insignificance of worldly objects, and a mind free from desires can be purified easily.

The purpose of spiritual practices, Parashurama, is to remove the three impurities. How much practice you need depends on how many you have. But commitment to practice comes only with *tivra mumuksha,* the intense desire for liberation. Without this, direct realization is impossible no matter how much you study or listen to a teacher or contemplate a philosophical truth.

A weak desire for liberation is useless. A transient impulse that arises from hearing about the glory of reality is not desire. It is excitement, a momentary curiosity that cannot inspire one to make a sincere effort. For that, one needs an intense desire, and the stronger the desire, the more quickly one attains the goal. This is what motivates an aspirant to wholehearted practice. And such motivation, along with unlimited courage to "carry through," is called absorption in sadhana. It is sparked when one realizes that compared to liberation everything else is trivial.

In other words, Parashurama, recognizing the worthlessness of worldly objects creates dispassion, or non-attachment, and the greater the dispassion, the more the yearning increases. Dispassion, in turn, fuels desire for liberation, and this desire leads to wholeheartedness, or absorption in practice. This is the major precipitating factor in attaining enlightenment.

P a r a s h u r a m a : Sir, what is this wholeheartedness or absorption in sadhana?

D a t t a t r e y a : It is to make this resolve with full confidence and determination: "No matter what happens, I will accomplish this.

This ought to be achieved and I can do it." Aspirants endowed with such single-minded resolution overcome every obstacle because the more they are absorbed in the practice, the sooner they attain the result.

P a r a s h u r a m a : First you said that the company of the saints is the major precipitating factor; then you talked about the grace of God; and now you speak of dispassion, desire, and whole-heartedness in spiritual practice. Which one is the primary method and how can I develop it? Please be more specific.

D a t t a t r e y a : This is the order: the company of the sages, God's grace, dispassion, and absorption in practice. Let me explain. It is human nature to constantly perform actions, and behind all action is the desire to attain happiness. Everyone makes an effort to attain whatever their concept of happiness is, but eventually they begin to fear that self-effort may not be enough. At this point aspirants turn to God, who is said to be almighty and who can fulfill all desires. They begin to read about God—questioning whether God exists, curious about how to pray, and wondering how much they can expect of God.

Seekers may also expect their good actions to help decrease life's problems and conflicts. But sometimes their charity, austerities, scriptural study, and other good deeds do not seem to bear commensurate fruit. They notice that often those who perform good karma suffer throughout life, while evil people are happy. Why? Unable to answer this question, they turn to the learned for advice.

Then, Parashurama, when aspirants listen to the wise extolling the greatness of God and spiritual practice, grace begins to descend; interest in the supra-mundane is quickened; and they begin to tread the path. But they must have some good karma from the past for this process even to begin.

Coming into the company of the wise is the most critical juncture in the soul's evolution, for it is at this point that one's true purpose as a human being begins to be fulfilled. The results of meritorious karma lead to *satsanga*, the company of the wise. Now seekers can listen to and associate with those who are further along the path, and their interest is kindled. They begin to perform spiritual practices. Through satsanga aspirants not only develop faith, they also learn how to draw the proper meaning from the scriptures. They learn about the absolute reality. In some cases aspirants may be taught to conceptualize the absolute through symbols and images, and in this way they attain the grace of God. This helps them cultivate indifference to sensory objects and awaken an ardent desire for enlightenment. This burning desire, in turn, helps develop unflagging determination to attain the goal, and now aspirants begin to listen to the confident inner voice that says, "I am going to do it. The goal can be attained and I will attain it."

69

This is the ground on which master and disciple meet. Aspirants become disciples, surrender to the master with perfect faith, and master teaches disciple about the non-dual state of reality. At first students comprehend this only theoretically, believing it rather than knowing it directly. But as they apply the techniques of meditation and contemplation the master has taught them, they realize the highest truth experientially.

Parashurama: Please explain how the *jñanis* [the knowers of truth] live in the world and remain unaffected by the bondage of karma if they perform actions after they are enlightened. Also, please explain why there are differences in the characteristics of the jñanis. Do they experience the truth differently, or is there simply a difference in the perfection of their knowledge? Are there various grades of jñanis? If there are, then why? Do they attain different levels of knowledge? Do some jñanis know more than others? Please explain this to me clearly.

Dattatreya: On the basis of the differing levels of their discriminatory ability, the number of remaining impurities, and, most important, the maturity of the knowledge they have attained, there are differences among the realized ones. These reflect the degree of their perfection of mind, not the degree of their knowledge.

The way they behave and the kind of lifestyle they lead is due to their innate characteristics.

But even after they have attained enlightenment, some innate qualities of mind persist. Knowers of the highest truth, those who have realized their true Self, remain aware of the truth while functioning in the world, while those who are unrealized forget the true Self and become lost in the world.

Enlightened sages may live in the world just like any ordinary person, exhibiting their usual tendencies while remaining unaffected by them. That is why there are saints and sages with different tastes, behaviors, and missions. These differences sometimes confuse ordinary people.

Realized beings can be light- or dark-skinned; their complexion in no way modifies their divine realization. The qualities of their mind, like the color of their skin, are the result of the interplay of the *gunas* [nature's intrinsic forces]. They bear no relation to their Self-conscious state. My son, the Self is entirely free from personality, which is part of prakriti [nature]. The jñanis do not identify with nature, and hence they do not identify with personality traits.

There are three levels of jñanis. The lowest order are those who have glimpsed the ultimate state but are not established in it. As long as they are meditating they remain absorbed in pure consciousness, but as soon as the focus of their awareness shifts back into the mindfield they identify with their limited selves—mind, senses, and body. They slip in and out of reality and go through the pleasant and unpleasant experiences of life.

The second order of jñanis are those who, through long and arduous discipline, have controlled their minds so well that their minds are fully purified. The yogis belonging to this category are centered in pure consciousness, but their bodies continue to function in the world. To an average person they might seem absentminded. Their minds are not "here," because they are fully present "there." Their stability of mind, however, still requires a conscious effort. They work in the world, but never under the pressure of their psychological defense mechanisms or biological instincts. They maintain their physical existence only to discharge their previous karmas, and how actively involved they are in the world depends on how they have decided to work out these karmas. But no matter what, they are not affected by life's circumstances.

The highest order of jñanis are completely unaffected by external objects. They remain fully established in their true nature without any effort. The intermediate jñanis are not "there" when they are "here"; the highest jñanis can be "here" and "there" simultaneously. They have attained such a high degree of mastery over their minds that they can focus on several objects at once, and to an average person they might seem scattered. Their daily activities flow naturally and spontaneously. They make no effort to do anything or to live in any particular way. Things happen by themselves; their bodies and minds simply get the credit for them. This is not to say that these jñanis live in a vacuum. They experience pleasure and pain and are aware of good and bad. But they consider these things to be no more than the objects of a dream.

They are like adults playing with children. As long as they have a body, they know they are still in the game and therefore act their parts. But they do not set new karmas in motion, because they have disengaged themselves internally from the world process. New desires cannot arise. They are free from liking and disliking, bondage, and even the concept of liberation. Thus they enjoy floating on the current of worldly life.

The life that we can observe of such enlightened sages is merely a shadow of their true being. They remain perfectly absorbed in supreme consciousness as they walk, eat, study, or work. They find no difference between samadhi and daily activities. They can engage in several activities at once without slipping from the blissful experience of non-dual samadhi. They are masters of both the external and internal worlds. In the drama of life they are both spectator and participant.

P a r a s h u r a m a : Sir, the qualities of a jñani are so personal, so subtle. How can they be observed by others? Can you tell me how to recognize a truly enlightened saint?

D a t t a t r e y a : It is extremely difficult to distinguish enlightened souls from ordinary men. Only the sage, himself, can describe his inner state or know the depth of his realization. But even so, a sharp student can instinctively recognize a jñani.

Generally, they can be identified by their philosophical insight, selflessness, and loving attitude toward others. Even an ordinary person can share these qualities to some degree, but they come naturally and spontaneously to realized beings. Fearlessness is also a marked virtue of true knowers, and this leaves them indifferent to name and fame even if they decide to undertake a public mission. They may work in the world quietly or openly; either way, they remain in divine consciousness, unaffected by praise or blame. But remember, my son, the highest jñanis often deliberately disguise themselves. Otherwise, worldly people would constantly make demands on them, saying things like "Please bless my business," "Grant me a child," "Help me find a husband." Only the most sincere students recognize enlightened sages intuitively and come to study at their feet.

It is hard to describe the exact signs of realized souls, but the characteristics and qualities described in the scriptures sometimes help novice seekers recognize them. For example, the highest knowers of truth can answer any spiritual question instantly without relying on books. A more subtle and definite indication that they are enlightened is their ability to solve spiritual problems without words. Their presence, itself, removes doubts and confusion. And sometimes, instead of answering a question directly, they may lead students to the source of their questions and then let them find the answer for themselves. After they have found the answer, an enlightened master simply confirms it.

Even so, my son, it is impossible to recognize an enlightened being through these subtle qualities until you have elevated your own intuitive awareness. First apply these standards to yourself.

Only after you have measured up to them are you competent to apply them to others.

These dialogues are but a fragment of those recorded by Parashurama's student, Haritayana, in *Tripura Rahasya*. Other scattered references to Parashurama's teachings can be found throughout the spiritual literature of India. But his most systematic and comprehensive instructions on philosophy and sadhana are found in *Parashurama-kapla-sutra*, which records his own words. This text is one of the most authoritative manuals on *shakti sadhana*, especially that of the *Sri Vidya* branch of shaktism, but it is not available in English. An in-depth explanation of its contents, however, can be found in *Hindu Tantric and Shakta Literature* by Teun Goudriaan and Sanjukta Gupta.

SHANKARACHARYA

Twelve hundred years ago in the village of Kaladi there lived a learned man named Shiva Guru and his wife, Araya Amba. Shiva Guru's life was dedicated to the study and teaching of the *Vedas* and *Upanishads,* and he was respected by all who knew him. Araya Amba worshipped God and served the *sadhus* (wandering monks) who frequently visited the village.

The couple was childless, and as they approached old age their sadness about this situation increased. Then one night, as they slept, both wife and husband dreamed that the sage Vyasa came to them and said, "A great soul has descended. Soon you will be blessed with a son of infinite wisdom and spiritual powers." In due time Araya Amba delivered a baby boy, whom the couple named Shankara.

Extraordinary qualities manifested in Shankara when he was quite young. He had a sharp intellect and a powerful memory. He seemed to know anything he was taught beforehand, and by the age of seven he had mastered the scriptures, a feat that ordinarily requires more than sixteen years of the most intense and demanding study.

Shankara also enjoyed discussing philosophical principles and spiritual practices with his father. One day, soon after having a long and serious discussion about the nature of the soul, birth, death, and the process of transmigration, Shiva Guru fell ill. And as Shankara watched him getting weaker and paler every day, he wondered how this physical weakness was affecting his father's inner being. What was actually experiencing the pain of sickness and old age—the body, the mind, or something else?

In due time Shankara witnessed his father's death. But while other members of the family wept in grief, Shankara remained motionless, lost in deep contemplation. He heard and saw nothing. People thought he was in shock, and some even thought he had gone insane. He remained immobile while everyone else prepared for the funeral. Hours passed. Then suddenly his consciousness shifted, his countenance changed, peace descended on him, and the knowledge that had just been revealed to him flowed into this verse:

> Water rises from the ocean,
> Turns into clouds and rain.
> No matter what shape and color it assumes,
> It flows on, and merges again with the ocean.
> Similarly, descended from the Atman,
> This *jiva*, the individual soul,
> Completes its journey and
> Merges again with Atman.

As he sang, Shankara raised his hands, and as he did so the consciousness of everyone present was elevated. Tears of joy washed away the sadness of everyone gathered there.

After this, Shankara lost his taste for worldly objects and pleasures, and when life had returned to normal he asked his mother's permission to renounce the world and move on with his spiritual pursuits. But Araya Amba was old and afraid. "You are my only son," she cried, embracing him. "You are the pupils of my eyes. To me, you are the blind man's stick. Don't abandon me, my son. I will not live for a moment without you." So Shankara did not push this matter further. He waited for his spiritual mission to take shape of its own accord.

One day a few years later, the boy went to the riverbank with his mother, and the pair joined many others from the village who were bathing in the river. Suddenly a crocodile appeared out of nowhere and caught Shankara in its jaws. Horrified, the onlookers shouted, threw stones, and hurled big sticks to frighten the reptile into letting go of his prey—but nothing worked. Holding tightly to the boy, it swam toward the deepest part of the river, pulling him beneath the surface several times. Shankara finally called out to his mother, "I'm on the verge of death—but this crocodile might spare me if you let me renounce the world for the sake of spiritual pursuit!"

His mother agreed and quickly began to pray: "For your sake, O Lord," she cried, "let this crocodile release my son." Instantly the reptile let go of the boy, and Shankara, only slightly injured, swam happily to shore. Touching his mother's feet, he bade her farewell— and caught between joy and sorrow, Araya Amba watched her son walk away.

And so Shankara began his journey to find the highest spiritual truth. He knew that the intellectual knowledge acquired from reading books and talking to scholars is not enough to unveil truth's mystery, for such knowledge, if it is devoid of direct experience, is like the unprotected flame of an oil lamp sitting under the open sky—even the tiniest ripple of emotional wind will blow it out. He also knew that just as a lamp needs oil, wick, and fire, intellectual knowledge requires a mentor as well as constant study, and a system of logic to support it. Otherwise, even after scholars have studied different texts and teachings, doubts still arise that lead to more confusion. Shankara did not want to become a mere pedant who spends his life in academic debates and finally dies without inner fulfillment. He wanted to go beyond intellect, and in order to do so he needed to find an experienced master.

The boy traveled far and wide and met many saints, sages, and yogis, but no one could satisfy him until at last he found the great sage and yogi Gaudapada. But Gaudapada was very old and wanted to be left in solitude, so he directed Shankara to his disciple, Govindapada, who was living in a monastery on the bank of the Narmada River in central India. This required a long and strenuous journey, but when Shankara finally arrived there, guru and disciple recognized each other at once. Almost immediately the young seeker received the highest initiation from his master, and by the age of twelve he was recognized as Govindapada's most learned and beloved disciple.

Govindapada knew that Shankara had an important spiritual mission and that when the time came he must leave the monastery in order to accomplish the goal for which he was destined. He had full confidence in the boy's intellectual knowledge, oratorical ability, and organizational capacities, but before he sent him on this mission he wanted to make sure that Shankara was fully prepared and that he had enough inner strength to withstand the blows that often fall on those who live in the world. He wanted to test the strength of Shankara's *sankalpa shakti*, his power of will and determination.

So one day Govindapada called his students together and explained that he was going to undertake a spiritual practice that would last several weeks. He gave strict instructions that no one should disturb him for any reason, and to Shankara he said, "You are in charge of the monastery. Unless I call someone or come out of my cottage, no one should enter." With that, he closed his eyes and went into deep samadhi.

It had been raining heavily, and a few days after Govindapada entered samadhi the river rose, flooding the whole area and threatening to sweep the monastery away. At first there were heated discussions about what to do and, especially, about how to save the master without disturbing him. But Shankara would not disobey his master's orders. One by one, many disciples left, explaining that it was Shankara's responsibility to cope with the emergency, not theirs. Most of them advised him to warn Govindapada or, at least, to transport his body to a safer place.

Shankara remained calm, waiting while the water rose. Not until the gate of the monastery was battered by the thrashing flood did he finally speak: "Control yourself, O River Narmada. Withdraw yourself lest you shrink to fit into my *kamandalu* [water pot], where you will remain until my master comes out of samadhi." Thus commanding the river, Shankara placed his water pot in the center of the gate, and to everyone's surprise the river receded instantly. Govindapada blessed Shankara with the highest gift of grace and wisdom when he resumed his normal state of awareness, and honored him with the title "acharya," which signifies a teacher who is an authority in himself and requires no further support from the scriptures. Thus Shankara came to be known as Shankaracharya.

Shortly after this Govindapada called Shankaracharya to him and said, "Your purpose here has been accomplished. Go and share the wealth that you have acquired with the rest of the world. May you be a light to yourself and a light to the world."

Shankaracharya then asked, "Have you any final words for me, *Gurudeva*? What exactly is the mission you want me to accomplish?"

Govindapada replied, "Be fearless. Let fearlessness radiate from you and dispel the fear in the hearts of others. Do not be a threat to others or consider anyone to be a threat to you.

"Deliver only the message of the sages that you have received either directly or from revealed scriptures like the *Vedas* and *Upanishads*.

"You must neither force nor manipulate others into following you. Instead, dedicate your life to the highest truth and let the magnetism of that truth pull people to you.

"Do not teach principles that you do not practice.

"Do not teach principles that you have found to be true in your direct experience but are contradicted by revealed scriptures. You must first resolve the discrepancies between your direct experience and scriptural revelations. Only then may you teach those principles.

"It is not important to teach all that you know; teach what people need to know and what they deserve to know.

"Guide them so that they improve their lives, become stronger, increase their capacities, gain deeper insight, and become worthy to receive and appreciate higher wisdom.

"Be a *parivrajaka* [a constant traveler]. Wherever you go, learn what people are missing and how it can be provided. Find a way to interact with people without hurting them.

"From now on, the ground is your bed, your arms are your pillow, the sky is the roof under which you sleep, fresh breezes are your fans, the sun and moon are your lamps, and dispassion is your life's companion. Without being burdened by any worldly possessions, be the emperor of the universe. May eternal peace be yours!"

With profound gratitude in his heart, Shankaracharya placed his head at the feet of his master, received his blessings, and left the monastery with only a water pot in his left hand and a staff in his right.

The eighth century A.D. was one of the darkest times in Indian history. The subcontinent was divided into many kingdoms and fiefdoms, and hundreds of cults and sects fought among themselves, attempting to impose their beliefs on others. Buddhism had been shaken to its core by extreme monasticism on the one hand and complicated ritualism and black magic on the other. In the same way, the sublime religion of Jainism was torn between asceticism and orgiastic tantric practices. Hinduism was mired in ritualism and excessive priestly practices. Scholars fought with one another to defend their philosophical positions, and people were confused about what to believe. Kingdoms rose and fell, and as power shifted from one faction to another, so did the prevailing religion. Followers of all faiths were disillusioned, tired of their priests selling their favors and taking advantage of them.

Seeing all this, Shankaracharya's heart was moved. He knew that the fewer the differences among people, the more peaceful the atmosphere would be. And he also knew that conflict could be overcome only if people came to realize the all-pervading, all-embracing absolute truth that underlies all diversities; only then could they bring about a qualitative change in their individual and collective lives. He realized that he must therefore build a strong philosophy—one that is practical, functional, and full of life. It must swallow all differences of creed, caste, and color, and through it people must be able to attain freedom from the guilt that religious leaders had created in the hearts of innocent believers. This philosophy must give them a chance to find and follow a path leading to freedom and independence.

As Shankaracharya contemplated the philosophy and practices that had been revealed to the sages and set forth in the *Vedas,* he realized that the path of *advaita,* the path of non-dual transcendental truth, is the only one that leads to perfect freedom and peace. And so he dedicated the fruits of his intellectual studies and spiritual practices to his fellow beings who were still involved with the world. Fully determined, he stood as firm as a mountain and delivered his message of non-dualism.

As the radiant young monk passed through villages and cities, people from all walks of life flocked to see him. It was not easy for Shankaracharya to face these crowds: not everyone came to learn from him and to share his wisdom. Those with pure hearts and honest minds heard what he said and understood what he meant; they took his teachings into their hearts and were soon transformed. But the clergy of the different sects and cults were first puzzled and then deeply disturbed as they noticed their followers dropping away. One by one, leaders from all religious groups began to challenge Shankaracharya. But just as the darkness cannot face the rising sun, they could not withstand the wisdom and spiritual power of this enlightened master. Like a powerful sun, he moved from one corner of India to another. And within a year or two, hundreds of scholars, religious dignitaries, and kings had become his students.

Without stopping for more than three nights at any one place, Shankaracharya walked from the tip of south India to Kashmir in the north, and from Gujarat on the west coast to Bengal and Puri on the east coast. During this long journey he encountered many scholars, yogis, and genuine seekers, as well as some impressive and clever hypocrites. Some highlights from this spiritual odyssey follow.

The holy city of Banaras (also known as Varanasi) has been a center of learning for centuries, and seekers from all over India have always longed to study with the masters of the various arts and sciences who live there. In Shankaracharya's time it was standard practice to introduce new systems of thought, philosophy, or spirituality by proving their validity in a public debate, and the most important of these were always held in Banaras. The secular rulers did not involve themselves in them, but others—particularly scholars—could always be expected to challenge new ideas and test them rigorously.

Shankaracharya arrived at the holy city with hundreds of followers trailing after him. One group of pandits welcomed him warmly, while another rejected him. A third group remained neutral, waiting to see how he would emerge from the scholarly battle that was imminent.

Shankaracharya seemed oblivious to the mixed reactions as well as to the impending debate. After bathing in the holy river, Ganga, he announced to his followers that he would go to the Vishvanatha Temple and offer his worship to Lord Shiva. This was exciting news because no one could understand how an adherent of non-dualism could worship God in a temple and yet teach others about the absolute reality without name and form. So people flocked to the temple. Many came to participate in the worship; but others simply wanted to see if Shankaracharya would participate in the ritual.

The ritual itself passed without incident: learned priests recited the Vedic hymns, and the devotees, including Shankaracharya, offered the routine ritual oblations. Then as the ritual ended, Shankaracharya rose with folded hands and spoke:

"Forgive me, O Lord," he said, "for three mistakes. First, I know and feel that You are all pervading and omnipresent, and yet

I have walked all the way here to worship You within the confines of this temple. Second, I know that there is only one non-dual truth, and thus there is no difference between You and me, yet I worship You as though You are different from me and outside of me. Finally, I know that this 'mistake' is simply my own mind-created concept—and yet I'm asking You to forgive me."

It was an astonishing performance—Shankaracharya had managed to offer his worship in an exact, traditional manner, but at the same time he had not strayed from his non-dualistic philosophy. The entire city fell at his feet. Some were impressed with his intellectual knowledge; others were enchanted with his spiritual wisdom and yogic powers; and some were simply overwhelmed by the fact that he had obtained so much wisdom at such a young age.

Shankaracharya held several discourses at different locations in Banaras. One, delivered under a pipal tree at Jñana Vapi, is particularly memorable because it gives us a glimpse of the traditional controversy about the path of action as opposed to the path of knowledge. In the realm of pure intellect, scholars maintain a sharp and uncompromising distinction between these two paths. But in the practical realm there is a beautiful balance between them. The following excerpt from Shankaracharya's discourse at Jñana Vapi shows how he created a bridge between the path of knowledge and the path of action.

"Jñana Vapi" means "well of knowledge." It is also the name of an area that lies behind the famous temple of Shiva in Banaras. For centuries philosophers, spiritual teachers, and religious leaders from all denominations have gathered there to discuss spiritual matters, and while Shankaracharya was in Banaras a spiritual conference was arranged to take advantage of his presence.

Someone from the audience started the discussion by saying, "According to you, sir, knowledge alone is the liberating force. The individual soul becomes bound to the cycle of birth and death as a result of its actions, and therefore in order to attain liberation we must stop performing actions. If that is the case, how are we to survive in the world?"

Shankaracharya replied, "It's true that ultimately knowledge is the only liberating force. But we cannot disregard our duties and follow the path of knowledge exclusively. In fact, there is no contradiction between the path of knowledge and the path of action. It is simply a matter of following a particular path at a particular stage of life. As long as we have not understood the nature of our internal world, the nature of our body, breath, mind, and soul, as well as our relationship with the external world, we must adhere to the path of action.

"But even though we are following the path of action, we must keep exploring its strengths and its weaknesses. We must also keep in mind the importance of discovering the inner essence of knowledge. The path of knowledge leads directly to Self-realization. But the path of action is in no way inferior to the path of knowledge, because it helps lead us to the path of knowledge.

"No one can survive without performing actions. But if we perform them without paying attention to the process of action, to the fruits of action, and to our attitude toward the fruits of action, then it entangles us in the snare of birth and death, and to the experiences that come between birth and death.

"Therefore, in the process of performing actions we must learn how to be skillful. Most of our actions are motivated either by the desire to gain something or by the fear that we will end up with something we do not want. Thus from the beginning our mind is focused on the fruits of actions, and when these fruits are achieved, we become attached to them. If the fruits are not achieved, we are disappointed and dissatisfied because of our intense desire and high expectations. In both cases, fear is the inevitable outcome. Either we fear losing the objects we have achieved through our efforts, or we fear that we will not achieve those objects.

"This fear cripples our creativity and destroys our peace of mind. If we are successful in our actions we cannot rest, because either we want more or we are afraid of losing whatever we have attained so far. If we are unsuccessful we are tortured by insecurity and fear of the future. So we must learn how to perform actions without getting attached to their fruits."

As Shankaracharya paused, someone from the audience interrupted: "Sir, even the most ignorant people have some idea of why they are trying to do something. Before attempting to act on the physical level, they think about what they want to accomplish. As the objective becomes clear, they decide on what means and resources to use to achieve that goal. As a result, they perform an action. Therefore, behind any action there is some degree of desire. The stronger the desire, the more energy is devoted to the task. Because of that desire, people place a value on the goal they want to achieve. And depending on how valuable that goal is, they decide which other tasks should be postponed or disregarded. Thus I do not understand how they can even begin to perform their actions without any desire or attachment to the fruits."

Shankaracharya replied, "I did not mean that we should set a task at random and start performing it without having a goal. There are three kinds of action. First, there are the compulsory actions we must perform for the sake of maintaining our existence: eating, bathing, and cleaning our houses and clothes are examples. These actions do not create karmic bonds.

"The second kind of actions are obligatory. We must perform them for the sake of maintaining healthy relationships with others. For example, we have karmic bonds with our closest relatives that can be loosened only by paying off our karmic debts to those who are connected with us. We must discharge our obligations to our parents, our children, our spouse, and even to our community and society. Although we are often tempted to underestimate the importance of these duties, deep in our heart we know that their call cannot be ignored without creating inner conflict and guilt. Self-condemnation results. Avoiding this is reason enough to perform these obligatory actions. They create karmic bonds only if they are not performed.

"The third category includes actions we perform with the intention of achieving specific objects for either temporal or so-called heavenly purposes. These actions are binding. It is the nature of the human mind not to be satisfied with performing only the first two kinds of actions—it takes them for granted. The sense of purposefulness, satisfaction, and fulfillment comes when we perform actions that are not mandatory. They are the challenge for us.

"In this area we must learn to perform our actions selflessly, lovingly, and skillfully, and then we must surrender the fruits of these actions to the higher truth. By so doing we minimize the effect of previous karmic bonds. In other words, attempting to attain freedom from the bondage of karma by performing actions is like using one thorn to extract another. Sooner or later we reach the realm where there are no more thorns. That is the realm of knowledge.

"Understanding that the purpose of performing actions is to extract the roots of previously performed actions gives us the strength we need to perform our actions selflessly and lovingly without becoming attached to their fruits—which then become like extracted thorns. Extract one thorn with another, and throw them both away. In this way we attain freedom from the bondage of karma.

"It is necessary to have the desire to extract the thorns of our previous actions. This is not an unhealthy desire—it motivates us to perform our actions. It is the desire to keep the fruits that is binding."

In this way Shankaracharya shared his knowledge and elevated the consciousness of those who studied and practiced under his guidance while he was in Banaras.

Shankaracharya had found two of his leading disciples—Padma Pada and Totaka—during his stay in Banaras, and when he left that city they were among the large number of students who walked with him to the Himalayas. According to the scriptures, many great sages in the past had done their practices and established centers of spiritual learning there, but when Shankaracharya arrived in the place where Rishikesh stands today he found nothing but the ruins of huts and cottages. A tribe of outlaws who did not believe in the higher values of life had taken over the entire region. And because their looting and killing had made pilgrimages to the Himalayan shrines dangerous, such pilgrimages were no longer undertaken.

When Shankaracharya arrived with his followers, the outlaws prepared to attack with bows and arrows, but according to legend, in the face of the power of love and non-violence that emanated from this great sage the warriors dropped their weapons. Even though they could not understand the profound teachings of the master, their violent energies were transformed and directed into constructive channels in a matter of a few days. And with their help Shankaracharya restored many of the beautiful and spiritually vibrant shrines in the foothills of the Himalayas. The most famous among these is Bharat Mandir.

At this time Shankaracharya founded the first of ten *dashanami* orders to prepare a spiritual community that would channel all its energies into the defense of righteousness. Initiates of this order do not necessarily need to be renunciates and live a monastic life—they can live as householders while they gradually prepare themselves for renunciation, and it is said that many of the early saints of this *dashanami* order came from the original band of outlaws. Even today, monks from other orders call initiates of this order "Shankaracharya's army."

Shankaracharya left most of his followers in what is now Rishikesh and, with only a few close disciples, began his journey to the high mountains. After several weeks he reached the famous shrine of Badrinath, where he stayed in a cave, known today as Vyasa Gupha, and taught the *Upanishads* and the *Brahma Sutra* to his students.

Then one day Shankaracharya told his disciples that it was time for him to cast off his body. Leaving orders that no one should disturb him, he withdrew into the cave, but soon a sage arrived and demanded to be taken to him. When the students told him that their master could not be disturbed because he had decided to cast off his body, the sage replied, "I know. That is why I'm here. I must see him."

With this the sage approached Shankaracharya, who knew at once that this was someone very special. "I am Vyasa," the sage said. "I have lived in this cave, and I have come to stop you from casting off your body."

"But my time is over," Shankaracharya replied. "Living beyond the assigned time is a violation of the law of nature."

"Do not worry," Vyasa said. "I will grant you sixteen more years from my own life. You have not yet completed your mission. You must write commentaries on the *Upanishads,* the *Brahma Sutra,* and the *Bhagavad Gita.* You must prepare your students so that they can continue the wisdom of the lineage. You must establish seats of learning in the four corners of India from where the knowledge of the *Vedas* can be disseminated. Only then can you return to your true abode."

Shankaracharya accepted Vyasa's gift humbly, made plans to return to the world, and, in the company of his disciples, began to walk toward the northern plains of India. Before reaching them, however, he stopped at a place which is now known as Joshi Matha, where he established his first seat of learning. Now popularly known as the northern monastery of Shankaracharya, it was first settled by learned brahmins from south India, who were assigned the job of meeting the educational and spiritual needs of the local people as well as the spiritual needs of pilgrims from all over the country. For twelve hundred years these brahmins have been serving as custodians of this northern seat, as well as many shrines in the high mountains.

Shankaracharya also established centers of learning in the east and west of India where seekers could study philosophical texts and be trained in the spiritual disciplines. But establishing such a center in the south proved difficult, because at that time southern India was the stronghold of a priestly class of brahmins who were involved largely in ritualistic practices. To make their position credible they had taken and popularized only those *brahmana* (ritualistic) sections of Vedic literature that supported their view. From this class of brahmins an intricate and logistically sophisticated philosophy, called Mimamsa, evolved that provided the philosophical ground for Vedic ritualism.

Shankaracharya knew that he faced a great challenge. And therefore while he was still in the Himalayas he decided to seek out Kumarila in the south and challenge him to a debate. Kumarila was the most respected Mimamsa scholar of his day, but he had also been schooled in the *Vedas* and *Upanishads,* and Shankaracharya knew that if he could convince this great man that the philosophy of *advaita,* non-dualism, was valid, the word would spread and his success would be assured. He would then be able to introduce the wisdom of the sages in the south.

Kumarila holds a significant place in the history of Indian philosophy. About five centuries before he and Shankaracharya were born, Buddhism had become the dominant philosophy and religion in India. Its monks had developed an unmatched system of logic and reasoning, and so Buddhism had become the most intellectually convincing path. But it had strayed from the original canonical texts, and the yogic and spiritual aspects of Buddha's teachings had been virtually replaced by elaborate rituals.

By Kumarila's time the monastic culture of Buddhism had taken hold of Indian society, and thousands of men and women swelled the monastic population. In the cities and villages monks walked from door to door with their begging bowls, asking for alms, and householders, who had a hard time feeding their own children, were forced to support them. Corruption thrived within the monasteries.

Society was silently begging for reformation, and Kumarila came forward. As a great scholar, orator, and man of repute, he openly confronted the social abuses in the monastic culture, but he was powerless against the existing system. On the few occasions that he gave discourses he was attacked by the Buddhists and lost the debates because he was not as well-trained in logic as they. Finally he decided that he must study Buddhist philosophy and logic to gain firsthand experience of its strengths and weaknesses in order to be able to refute it effectively.

Kumarila wanted to study at Nalanda, a famous Buddhist university, but to be admitted he had to convert to Buddhism and be ordained as a Buddhist monk. Only then was he allowed to study with the famous teacher Dharmapala. This turned out to be an ordeal: every day Kumarila experienced the humiliation and pain of working within a system designed to refute and condemn the views of others. As a learned scholar and practitioner of the wisdom of the sages he was capable of presenting a correct and meaningful interpretation of the *Vedas* and *Upanishads,* but he was not allowed to do so, because the views of other philosophies and faiths were censored at the university.

Several years passed. Then one day while he was sitting at the back of the classroom tears began to flow from his eyes as he listened to erroneous interpretations of the *Vedas* and the *Upanishads* along with unreasonable criticism of them. The teacher noticed his tears and asked what was wrong. "I feel sad for myself and pity for all of you," Kumarila replied quietly. "You do not know the essence of Vedanta, and because of your prejudice, you are condemning the sublime wisdom it contains."

Enraged, the teacher ordered his students to seize Kumarila, take him to the roof, and throw him off. The students obeyed, but just as they were about to throw him over the edge Kumarila raised his hand and said, "If I have sincerely studied and practiced the wisdom of the sages, and if my faith is pure, then I will remain unharmed."

The students pushed him from the roof—and were astonished to see him land, unhurt except for the loss of one eye. Kumarila walked away safely, but he could not understand why the power of his faith had not protected him completely. So he went to his former teacher, the man who had taught him the *Vedas* and *Upanishads,* and asked why he had lost an eye.

"Because you used the word 'if,' my son," the wise man replied. "On this path there is no room for 'if.' Deep down in your heart there was a seed of doubt, and it was reflected on your tongue in the word 'if.' The result was only partial protection. The perfection of the power of will, determination, and faith was compromised."

From this time on, however, Kumarila was able to defeat his opponents in debates and teach the path of the sages. He wrote his famous work *Shloka Varttika,* and prepared intellectually and spiritually powerful students such as Prabhakara and Mandana Mishra. But most people were not yet ready for non-dualistic Vedanta, so he continued to teach Mimamsa, the path of rituals, and his teachings did not include the spiritual disciplines. In this sense, Kumarila's noble work was limited to the field of religion.

When Kumarila reached old age he resolved to purify himself from the guilt he felt for having cheated his Buddhist teacher. According to his high ideals there were no sins worse than lying to one's teacher, learning from him, and then denouncing both teacher and teachings. So he journeyed to Allahabad, at the confluence of the Ganga and Yamuna Rivers, and after taking a bath in the Ganga he made a specially prepared, slow-burning fire on the riverbank and sat in it. Then with voluntary control and conscious awareness he began to gradually leave his body as the fire consumed him from the lower extremities to the upper regions of his body. This process took days.

This was taking place just as Shankaracharya was leaving the Himalayas for the plains of India to seek out Kumarila. By the time he reached him, part of the great man's body had already been consumed by fire and Kumarila could hardly speak. "It is too late for me to help you, O Acharya," he said in a weak voice. "Go to Mandana, my student, in the south. His knowledge is equal to mine. Exchange ideas. If you can convince him of the validity of the philosophy and practices you teach, he will become your disciple and be instrumental in your mission. May God bless you and help you accomplish your task." Thus this great man left his body, and Shankaracharya began his journey to the south.

Like his master, Mandana was a great teacher, and hundreds of students studied at his ashram under his guidance. As legend has it, when Shankaracharya was still some distance from Mandana's village he asked directions of some women who were fetching water at the well. They glanced at one another, and then one of them said, "You are on the right road. Mandana's village is still a few miles from here. When you reach it, you will not need to ask where he lives. When you find parrots and myna birds discussing and debating whether this world is real or unreal—know that place to be Mandana's ashram."

Eager to hear birds discussing metaphysics, Shankaracharya and his companions found the place even more impressive than the women had led them to expect. From a distance the travelers heard young students reciting mantras from the *Vedas*. The air was fragrant, the sky being filled with trails of smoke rising from ritual fires. The altars were decorated with streamers of mango leaves and canopies of banana plants, and a peaceful energy emanated from yantras and mandalas made of colored rice and barley flour. Cows greeted them quietly, while their excited calves danced in welcome. Parrots and myna birds greeted the guests, saying, "Welcome to all of you."

Mandana Mishra greeted Shankaracharya and his followers respectfully, and asked why they had come. Shankaracharya first told him that Kumarila had left his body in the slow fire on the bank of the Ganga, and then he expressed his desire to discuss spiritual matters with him, especially the true intent of the scriptures.

Mandana responded, "I am a householder, and my first duty is to perform the after-death rites for my guru. You are most welcome here, and I will gladly discuss anything you wish from the scriptures, but you must wait until I have completed the rites."

Shankaracharya agreed to the delay, and Mandana began his task. Meanwhile news of the coming debate spread quickly. People flocked to Mandana's village to be present, and by the time the after-death rites were completed, preparations had been made for the debate and the audience was ready. All that remained was to find a competent judge to preside—which was not easy, because the judge had to be at least as learned as the two great scholars. The only one who qualified was Bharati, Mandana's wife, and she accepted the task humbly. What follows are fragments of a debate that continued for days.

B h a r a t i : In respect to knowing the unknown, in respect to seeing the unseen, and in respect to staying in tune with the law of the Divine, what is the highest and most reliable authority?

M a n d a n a : The *Vedas*.

S h a n k a r a c h a r y a : The *Vedas*.

B h a r a t i : What is the intent of the *Vedas*?

M a n d a n a : Rituals are the true intent of the *Vedas*.

S h a n k a r a c h a r y a : Knowledge is the true intent of the *Vedas*.

B h a r a t i : How do you justify your view that rituals are the true intent of the *Vedas*? How do rituals help one attain the highest goal of life?

M a n d a n a : All the contents of the *Vedas* as revealed in the scriptures can be divided into two major categories. Certain sections of the *Vedas* describe facts regarding the nature of unmanifest, absolute truth; the nature of the manifest world; the place of human beings in this creation; and the facts related to birth, death, and transmigration. Other sections of the *Vedas* set forth rules and methods for living in the world, for interacting with others, for performing one's duties, and for attaining the highest goal of life in successive stages.

It is important to know who created this world, how it evolved, what the highest truth is, and what we are. But it is even more important to know how to participate in the process of creation that

23

has been set in motion by the higher forces of nature. It is important to know how to follow the rhythm of nature and thereby establish harmony between individual and collective consciousness, between the microcosm and the macrocosm. Rituals as described in the *Vedas* are the way to participate in the activities of nature and to forge a link between them.

Rituals show us how to enact the process that takes place in nature—the constant process of giving and receiving, materializing and dematerializing, gaining and losing, creating and destroying. Vedic rituals are the way to do this. By offering material objects into the fire, we witness the process of materializing and dematerializing. By giving an offering at the end of rituals, we familiarize ourselves with the principle of gain and loss. In compliance with Vedic teachings, at the end of each ceremony the physical structure in which the ceremony was conducted is also offered to the fire, and this unveils the mystery of creation and destruction.

S h a n k a r a c h a r y a : Rituals are like blankets that veil the truth. They are nets to trap our intellect. They force us to confine our consciousness to the superficial values of the manifest world. The thinking of those who believe only in the value of ritual practices becomes confined to this little world. The subtle thoughts of the mind and the tender feelings of the heart become outward-oriented, and such people begin to believe that everything can be accomplished with the help of the rituals they perform.

Because rituals involve material objects, and because they are systematic and have a defined goal, the performer's expectations grow and become vivid. And when the expected results don't happen, as is usually the case, they are disappointed. In order to cope with the disappointment, they try to discover what went wrong in the ritual. Then the interpreter, who is usually a priest, takes advantage of the situation and puts the entire blame on the performer, saying things like, "You did not do it with the right attitude of mind; you did not follow the exhortations correctly; you did not give the appropriate love offering to the officiating priests." Such explanations create and perpetuate guilt in those who perform the ritual.

The ancient parts of the revealed scriptures tell us that the original rituals were a simple means of channeling one's devotion toward the Divine. They did not require help from priests and clergy. Now, however, aspirants want their rituals to be performed by priests. And in order to show off their expertise and impress their clients, these priests elaborate on the rituals, and this causes them to become riddled by dogma and superstition.

Then, as such practices continue, it becomes a fad to make ritual performances glamorous, and gradually more advanced and elaborate ritualistic practices are introduced into the ceremony. At this stage, rituals are no longer a means of either channeling devotional feelings or fueling spiritual unfoldment—they have become social events, a form of entertainment, a way to display status; they have degenerated into cultural activities. But even before this has happened they had little or no spiritual value.

M a n d a n a : If rituals are meaningless, then why do the *Vedas* advocate them?

S h a n k a r a c h a r y a : The subtle essence of rituals lies in their symbolic or contemplative meanings, and these inner meanings must be brought closer to our day-to-day life. In order to assimilate the spiritual value of rituals, we must not only perform them, we must also live with the message that they convey: non-attachment, selflessness, and remaining free from identifying oneself with the objects of the world.

M a n d a n a : Do all rituals have symbolic meanings?

S h a n k a r a c h a r y a : Yes. Rituals are like maps of spiritual practices. Seekers cannot reach the goal pictured on the map by simply reading the map and drawing it over and over. In the beginning, in order to become familiar with the spiritual map, they may practice rituals, but if they do not know how to internalize them, even if they have become good cartographers they will not become adept in spiritual experience.

Ritualistic practices are a means of keeping busy in the external world while maintaining a relatively less worldly awareness. Rituals also give people an opportunity to interact with one another in a relatively loving environment. But if they come to a ritual with their worldly attitudes and habits, they will fight even at the altar. Therefore inner transformation, which requires knowledge and the direct experience of truth, is the only way to attain Brahman—the highest good, the non-dualistic, absolute truth.

As the debate progressed, Mandana's attitude toward Shan-karacharya changed. He stopped arguing with him for the sake of argument and began to make genuine inquiries because he wanted to learn.

On the seventh day, Bharati declared Shankaracharya the winner of the debate and Mandana surrendered himself at Shankar-acharya's feet. But then, after giving her judgment in Shankar-acharya's favor, she said to him: "Yours is only half a victory since I, the wife of Mandana, have not yet been defeated." Thus it became her turn to debate Shankaracharya:

B h a r a t i : What is knowledge? Are there different grades and degrees of knowledge? And what is attained through knowledge?

S h a n k a r a c h a r y a : Knowledge is the direct experience of the highest truth: Brahman, absolute non-dual awareness. When knowledge is attained, nothing remains to be attained. Nothing remains unknown. When they receive such knowledge, aspirants become established in this state, which is called Self-realization: they know their true Self and realize that it is the Self of all. And by thus knowing their own essence, such seekers become fearless. Doubt, conflict, and insecurity vanish. Their clear understanding and direct experience make them secure, and they remain tranquil even in the face of the grimmest disasters.

B h a r a t i : There seems to be no place for worldly knowledge in all this. Are worldly knowledge and absolute knowledge mutually exclusive? Is one completely meaningless in the light of the other?

Shankaracharya: In the scriptures, knowledge of worldly objects is called *apara vidya,* and knowledge of the absolute truth is called *para vidya.* Those who have not attained the direct experience of the highest truth do not see the connection between lower knowledge and higher knowledge, while those blessed with higher knowledge not only see this connection, they also have a better understanding of worldly existence.

This point can be made clear by an example. When we are standing in a valley we cannot see the entire valley or what lies on the mountain peaks. But the higher we climb, the wider our field of vision becomes and the better our understanding of the valley and everything below as well as everything level with our eyes. Those who reach the summit can see everything. Thus the knowledge of both mountain and valley is included in the knowledge of the peak.

Bharati: Is it possible to skip lower knowledge and gain higher knowledge directly?

Shankaracharya: It is possible, but extremely difficult. To climb to the summit of truth, aspirants have to begin the journey from the point where they are presently standing. If they are struggling with day-to-day existence, their consciousness is completely occupied by the idea of self-preservation. If their actions are motivated by desire, attachment, fear, anger, greed, and so on, they have little chance of going beyond the mundane; it will be impossible for them to climb to the summit without first meeting and overcoming these worldly challenges.

In order to be practical and systematic, seekers must understand what this external world is, how the objects of the world relate to them, and what their exact place is in the scheme of creation as well as in their family, society, and culture. This knowledge will make it possible for them to live a healthy life and make good use of their time and energy. The more that aspirants know of the ways of the world, the more successful they are while they live in the world.

At the same time, most of the obstacles to spiritual endeavors are created either directly by the external world or indirectly by our attitude toward the external world. Aspirants spend most of their time and energy trying to remove these obstacles, and this leaves very little time for spiritual practices. Most of these obstacles are directly connected to what they expect from the objects they gain through their actions, or what they expect from the people they love or from those who claim to love them. When they know the nature of worldly objects and worldly love they no longer have these expectations, and therefore neither this world nor their so-called loved ones can disappoint them.

When they are no longer disappointed by anyone or anything, they will have no complaints; a mind free from complaints is an abode of peace; and a peaceful mind is naturally inclined to turn inward and explore the nature of higher truth. That is why the scriptures say that with the help of lower knowledge one attains freedom from the fear of death, and with the help of higher knowledge one becomes immortal.

B h a r a t i : What is the difference between attaining freedom from the fear of death and gaining immortality?

S h a n k a r a c h a r y a : Attaining freedom from the fear of death means attaining freedom from the pain caused by fear of all kinds. To those who are ignorant, death seems to be the most fearsome phenomenon, and therefore it is the most painful experience. The fear of death arises from the thought "I am going to lose everything." Throughout life, human beings work hard and continually identify with the successes and failures brought about by their actions. But ultimately all their actions and related successes and failures are centered around themselves. The more concrete the image of their self as mere body and ego, the more terrifying the thought of losing the body. At the moment of death they are appalled by the idea of losing everything. That is why even those in severe pain do not want to die.

However, those who are familiar with the laws of nature—which includes the law of change, death, decay, and destruction—can overcome their attachments and false identifications and go through a smooth transition at the time of death. And the smoother the transition, the smoother the entry into the world the next time. The weaker their attachment to worldly objects, the more freedom they have to leave the body voluntarily.

Everyone dies—both those who try to cling to objects and those who voluntarily leave things behind. The difference is that the first group is forced out, while the second leaves willingly. The same principle applies at the time of conception: some are forced to be born, and others enter a body of their own volition. Those in the first group drown in the cycle of births and deaths; those in the second group incarnate. For those in the first group, birth and death are bondage; for those in the second group, birth and death are part of the divine will, the divine game; the individual simply plays an assigned role in the process.

Freedom from the fear of death, however, does not mean that seekers will never die; it means that they have raised their consciousness to the level at which they are free to exit from the body and enter a new body at will. Attaining immortality, on the other hand, means gaining knowledge of the immortal Self and allowing consciousness to be fully established in that. This not only imparts freedom from the fear of loss and gain, it also grants a state of infinite and eternal bliss.

Then, with the direct experience of eternal bliss, aspirants no longer crave sense pleasure. They no longer feel lonely and empty; they enjoy their perfection regardless of their external circumstances. They have become masters of the mind and senses, and for them satisfaction and happiness lie not in worldly objects but in their own decision to be satisfied and happy. Such a state cannot be disturbed as the objects of the world come and go.

B h a r a t i : Why are people attracted to worldly objects and sense pleasures?

S h a n k a r a c h a r y a : Objects in the external world awaken the *vasanas* [the subtle impressions of past experiences that are hidden deep in the mindfield]. And because the mind and the senses tend to seek the same pleasures, over and over, the mind projects its sense of pleasure upon those objects and allows itself to be distracted by them. Objects by themselves have no power to attract the mind; instead, the mind projects attractiveness onto objects and then becomes attracted to them.

B h a r a t i : How were these vasanas created in the first place? What caused the mind to gain the experience stored in the form of vasanas, and consequently to subject itself to this long, almost unending, chain of experiencing pleasure and pain?

S h a n k a r a c h a r y a : The mind begins this process under the influence of *avidya* [ignorance] and becomes so enmeshed that it does not know how to free itself.

B h a r a t i : How does the mind come under the influence of avidya in the first place?

S h a n k a r a c h a r y a : Avidya is beginningless. Therefore this process is also beginningless.

B h a r a t i : How discouraging! But please explain the relationship between ignorance and Brahman—your non-dual, absolute truth. Is ignorance a complete and independent category of reality? If so, then you must accept that there are two sets of reality: Brahman and ignorance. If ignorance is not an independent category of reality, then it must be dependent on or at least secondary to Brahman. This makes Brahman a qualified truth, which therefore compromises its pure absoluteness. And if ignorance is not a category of existence at all, then such a non-existent principle cannot have much influence over anything, including the mind. Please clarify your position.

S h a n k a r a c h a r y a : Ignorance as such does not exist. Therefore it is neither an independent category of reality nor a category dependent on Brahman. It is an illusion. Mistaking one thing for something else, such as mistaking a rope for a snake, is an example of ignorance.

B h a r a t i : It seems incomprehensible to me that ignorance, which is completely non-existent and illusory, can gain so much control over Brahman, the pure truth, that Brahman gets caught and becomes subservient to this illusion. In answer to this question you will say, as do all the scriptures, that this is "the greatest mystery," beyond the realm of verbal question and answer. Therefore I drop the question altogether. But I would like to know what the mind and the senses are searching for in the external world as they go through pleasant and unpleasant experiences.

Shankaracharya: The mind and the senses are searching for joy and bliss, but they are looking in the wrong direction. They mistake mere pleasure for true bliss. And as soon as they realize their mistake, they are disappointed by the transitory nature of the sensory pleasure they have just received. Even so, they repeat this process again, hoping that the next experience will be more profound and longer lasting. But again, as always, they are disappointed and frustrated.

Bharati: Why are the mind and senses so interested in finding bliss, or even pleasure?

Shankaracharya: Bliss is an intrinsic characteristic of Atman, the soul. But in the outward journey of life the soul has lost—or at least forgotten—its intrinsic characteristic. And without the experience of bliss, human beings feel empty and dissatisfied.

Bharati: You say that there is something called bliss, which is intrinsic to one's inner being, that the mind and senses are searching for it, and that regardless of whether or not they are searching in the right direction, at least the intention of the mind and the senses is correct. How can you talk about this with such certainty when you have little worldly experience, especially with regard to sex? That is one of the most powerful drives and greatest sources of pleasure.

At this Shankaracharya was quiet. Then he said, "Give me six months. I will gain direct experience of the world and then come back and talk to you on the basis of that." Bharati agreed, and so without reaching any conclusion, the assembly was adjourned.

Shankaracharya, accompanied by his two closest students, Padma Pada and Totaka, went to the high mountains, where he made plans to leave his body, enter another body in which he would gain worldly experience, and then return to his own body. Padma Pada and Totaka were instructed to preserve his body in the snow and guard it until he returned. In the yogic tradition this process is called *parakaya pravesha.*

In his subtle body Shankaracharya searched for an appropriate physical body in which to gain worldly experience, and eventually he found a king in Bengal who had just died unexpectedly. The entire court was in mourning and preparations were underway for the funeral. But suddenly there was a miracle: as Shankaracharya's spirit entered the corpse, the king came back to life.

It took a while for Shankaracharya to orient himself in the king's body and become familiar with the people and the routine around him. His subjects were puzzled because the king did not behave in his usual manner, but they assumed that he had been in a coma that had somehow affected his memory and his personality. Gradually, however, Shankaracharya assumed all of the king's former responsibilities. As a public figure, he began to gain firsthand experience in governing and all the headaches the head of a country goes through. In his private life he adjusted to all the pleasures that attend royalty—dance, music, food, women, and other sensory delights. In the beginning Shankaracharya was aware of his true identity and of his purpose in entering the king's body, and he enacted the drama consciously. But gradually he began to lose that awareness, and rather than remain a spectator, he began to participate. As the sense of "enjoyer" grew, the awareness of "pure witness" began to fade, and there came a point at which he no longer knew that he was Shankaracharya. He had fully identified with the king, and consequently he was trapped—internally and externally.

Weeks passed, and then months. High in the Himalayas, Padma Pada and Totaka began to wonder why their master was so long in returning. Worried, Padma Pada decided to find out, and in a state of deep meditation he found his master ruling a kingdom and enjoying its pleasures. He tried to communicate with him, but there was no response. So he went to Bengal to meet his master in person, leaving Shankaracharya's original body in Totaka's custody.

But Shankaracharya was now a king, and gaining access to him was not easy. It was not until Padma Pada discovered that this king was very fond of poetry and had a great respect for poets that he was able to pass himself off as an accomplished bard and offer his services to the king. This gained him access to the court, but when he arrived he was shocked when the king did not recognize him. What was worse, the king did not even understand the profound but veiled remarks that Padma Pada made to reveal his own identity and remind Shankaracharya of who he really was.

Forced to be more direct, Padma Pada began to recite a poem (recast here as prose): "What has happened to you, O cave dweller? You have forgotten who you are, whence you have come, why you have come, and your destination. You have identified yourself with this body. Thus, today you feel that you are a certain number of years old. Not knowing truly who you are, you find yourself sometimes happy, sometimes miserable. Losing the awareness of your true identity, you depend on external objects to make you happy. Your expectations have grown to the point at which—in spite of having lost your teeth, the light of your eyes, your power of hearing, and the hair on your head—you run after the mirage of sense pleasures. One by one, the senses are saying goodbye to you, but cravings persist and you, the victim, do not know what to do or where to go. O master of senses! Master of mind! O knower of Brahman! Light of my soul! Come out of this dream. Open your eyes. Recognize yourself and know who I am."

This poem awakened Shankaracharya from his kingly slumber. He rewarded the poet richly and then, pretending to have a headache, went to the king's chambers and left the king's body in the same way that he had entered it. He then returned to the high mountains, reentered his original body, joined his students, and returned to south India to continue his debate with Bharati on the basis of direct experience.

B h a r a t i : When you entered the body of the king, what did you notice?

S h a n k a r a c h a r y a : It was like moving into a new cottage. The body had to be trained and adjusted to the mind and consciousness that had entered it.

B h a r a t i : But how did you gradually lose your true self-identity? Did your mind also adjust to the habits of the king's body?

S h a n k a r a c h a r y a : Yes. Because of a strong identification with the king's body, the mind became affected by the bodily *samskaras* of the king. And the more that identification grew, the more Self-awareness receded. The lesson I learned is that if one does not pay attention, then the body and mind will interact with each other almost blindly, and this interaction will lead those who are ignorant into utter confusion.

Shankaracharya went on to explain the nature of desire, of attachment, and of the process by which the body-mind organism evolves from the most subtle principle, known as *kama* (primordial desire). He also explained the divine nature of kama, which is an intrinsic aspect of divine will. It is from this divine will, known as *ichccha shakti,* that the power of knowledge and the power of action spontaneously evolve. As the individual soul begins its outward journey, it keeps moving farther away from the divine nature of kama, and as it does so, kama turns into worldly desires and cravings. On the other hand, this same principle of kama, if understood properly, can unveil the mystery of creation, maintenance, and destruction. Thus kama can open the door to enlightenment, but if it is not understood properly, it can propel a soul into the path of worldly transmigration.

Discussions about the oneness of the divine force and the absolute truth—and the evolution of this force into the power of will, the power of knowledge, and the power of action—lead in the direction of shaktism, and more specifically, to the sublime philosophy and practices of *Sri Vidya*. The tradition does not usually discuss this subject, and Shankaracharya does not mention this aspect of his teachings in his commentaries on the *Upanishads*, the *Brahma Sutra*, or the *Bhagavad Gita*. Nevertheless, *Sri Vidya* is the culmination of that tradition; it has been most profoundly described in the text *Saundaryalahari* (The Wave of Beauty and Bliss). Bharati asked many more questions, and Shankaracharya answered them to her satisfaction. Finally she too accepted him as her spiritual master. And thus wife and husband were ordained. After the initiation Bharati retained her name, but Mandana Mishra was renamed Sureshvaracharya.

Soon after this, Shankaracharya heard that his mother had fallen ill and might soon leave her body. He knew she would want to see him before she died, so he began his journey to her side.

People often waited along the road to greet Shankaracharya as he passed by, and one day as he approached a village he saw an elderly couple waiting for him with their only son. This young man had never spoken and seemed to be autistic. His parents, worried about how he would survive after their death, had brought him to Shankaracharya in hope of a cure. They prostrated themselves at his feet. Shankaracharya looked keenly at the son. "Have you been giving your parents a hard time?" he asked. "Why don't you communicate with others?"

To everyone's astonishment the young man said, "This world is not worth the trouble of communication, so I keep quiet."

Shankaracharya addressed the parents: "This is a wise soul," he said. "The time has come for him to unfold all his potentials. He belongs to me. You had the privilege of bringing him into the world. Now withdraw your attachment to him. The world is waiting." The parents gratefully complied, and the young man was ordained as a renunciate and given the name Hastamalaka, which means "He who sees the whole truth like a small fruit in the palm of his hand."

When Shankaracharya arrived at his birthplace he found his mother counting her last breaths. Happy and at peace at the sight of him, she left her body in the presence of her enlightened son. But this forced Shankaracharya once again to meet a challenge from a society locked into rigid orthodoxy.

According to the customs of the time, once they took a vow of renunciation aspirants were no longer permitted to associate with their relatives. But not only had Shankaracharya visited his mother, he also planned to perform her funeral rites. Orthodox brahmins were shocked and adamantly opposed this. Some of them went so far as to say that because the woman had died in the presence of her son, a monk who had renounced the world, both she and her funeral were inauspicious. Many refused to have anything to do with either her funeral or Shankaracharya.

Unperturbed by the commotion, Shankaracharya prepared his mother's funeral pyre and cremated her in front of her house. Then he raised his hands and said, "May this be my curse or my blessing: From this day forward the community that abandoned my mother and me will cremate their dead in front of their homes. May it be a permanent practice for generations to come." Those who heard him suddenly understood that all social and cultural practices are ultimately manmade, and that if they are accepted rigidly, without room for reformation, society suffocates. Realizing their ignorance, they asked Shankaracharya to explain why he had violated the rules of renunciation.

Shankaracharya replied, "You do not renounce your family and relatives merely for the sake of renouncing them. You renounce your little world, your family, in order to find a bigger world, the whole of humanity, and ultimately to find the highest spiritual truth. You accomplish this grand goal by renouncing not your family but your attachment to your family, for the stronger your attachment to your own family and relatives, the less open you are to the rest of your fellow beings.

"On the path of renunciation you are not required to be ungrateful to those who have helped you. The woman I have cremated was my mother. Why then is it wrong to express my love and gratitude to her? It is hypocrisy to claim that I have nothing to do with anyone anymore. The only thing that matters is love. Love is the greatest law. No other law can surpass it."

With this, the people of the community humbly accepted Shankaracharya as their spiritual guide and adopted the practice of cremating their dead in front of their homes.

By this time Shankaracharya had established a monastery in each of the four corners of India and appointed a disciple to head each of them. One is in south India (either the monastery at Kanchi or the one at Shringeri; there is controversy on this point), one is on the west coast at Dwarika, one is on the east coast at Puri, and the fourth, now known as Joshi Matha, is in the Himalayas. The head of each of these monasteries is given the title of "Shankaracharya."

According to oral tradition, however, Shankaracharya himself spent most of his time at a fifth monastery, Karvirpitham, in the Kolhapur region of central India. This is the center where, according to legend, he appointed Bharati as his fifth representative, and the lineage connected to this monastery is called Bharati, which literally means "lover of knowledge." According to some sources this tradition gets its name from its exclusive emphasis on the knowledge of Brahman; according to other sources, this tradition is called Bharati after Shankaracharya's first successor.

Knowledge is all that is needed to belong to the Bharati tradition. In this context "knowledge" means *mokshakam jñanam,* "the knowledge that liberates"—which is the only true knowledge. In the lineage of the other four monasteries the senior disciple of the previous teacher is usually designated as the successor. In the tradition of Bharati, however, direct experience of the wisdom of the sages is the criterion one must meet to be worthy of holding the post. And there have been times in the past when this seat of learning has remained vacant for decades because no one could meet that requirement. Candidates for the position at Karvirpitham must demonstrate competence by facing the challenges posed by a learned assembly of scholars, saints, and yogis. They must be well versed in all systems of philosophy, but their knowledge must be experiential as well as theoretical, and they must be capable of teaching and personally guiding aspirants in any path that suits them. They must honor all traditions and be capable of resolving the apparent contradictions between them. They must not identify with any particular caste, race, community, or nationality. They must be fearless and must not be a threat to anyone. Ultimately, only those who have attained perfect freedom are fit to fill this post. (The qualifications and prerequisites for holding the seat at Karvirpitham are described in the text *Mathamnaya*.) Unlike those in the other subtraditions that sprang from Shankaracharya, the adepts of the Bharati subtradition travel freely. Most of them prefer to remain unknown to the public, and they never involve themselves in religious matters.

After a long, long gap, this post was filled in the early twentieth century by a great and learned scholar, Dr. Kurtkoti. Swami Rama of the Himalayas, the founder of the Himalayan International Institute, succeeded him in 1949, but after several years he renounced this position to be with his master in the mountains.

Shankaracharya delivered the message of the sages as found in the *Vedas* and the *Upanishads*. He emphasized knowledge, but he also maintained a harmonious balance between karma (action) and *bhakti* (love and devotion). On one hand, he taught us how to go beyond the realm of maya and attain the pure non-dual knowledge of the absolute Brahman. On the other hand, he showed us how to adjust to the idea of a personal, or personified, God as a stepping-stone to the realization of the absolute Brahman that is nameless and formless.

With the passage of time, however, Shankaracharya's message fell into the hands of academics, scholars, and philosophers who were not connected with his lineage. Different interpretations of his teachings arose, and in time only one component was stressed: knowledge alone. This eventually turned into cold intellectualism. Then in later years other philosophers and scholars emerged who either supported Shankaracharya's teachings or introduced a slightly different philosophy along similar lines. In order to distinguish themselves from Shankaracharya's system, they developed systems of logic to support their own views and taught only the portions of the *Vedas* and *Upanishads* that supported their ideas. And they used these references, in conjunction with their own commentaries and interpretations, to undermine the authenticity of Shankaracharya's views.

To counter this, many students in Shankaracharya's lineage developed their own highly sophisticated system of logic and reasoning known as advaita Vedanta. Thus in the system of philosophy expounded by Shankaracharya a high degree of scholasticism has emerged. In response, some learned adepts of Shankaracharya's tradition have from time to time reintroduced the practical aspects of his message in order to establish once again his perfect balance between philosophy and practice.

VIDYARANYA YATI

According to the Shankaracharya tradition, the great sage Vidyaranya Yati was born into a learned and prosperous brahmin family in south India at the beginning of the fourteenth century. He received the best education available at that time and became an expert in grammar, medicine, astronomy, mathematics, poetics, political science, and even architecture. He also committed himself to spiritual studies and disciplines, assiduously following his family's tradition of the *shrotriya brahmin* (those who are well versed in Vedanta) from early childhood. In such families the study of the *Vedas* and *Upanishads* as well as certain ascetic practices are passed on from generation to generation. Taking advantage of this tradition, Vidyaranya embarked on an intense practice of the *gayatri* mantra at the age of eleven, when he received *yajñopavita* (the sacred ceremonial thread).

In his early adulthood Vidyaranya and a group of scholars organized, restored, commented on, and translated many Vedic scriptures. And in addition to being a prolific writer, he was also the teacher of two kings, Harihara and Bukka Rai, brothers, who jointly ruled the same empire. How great a sage Vidyaranya was can be seen not only through his works but also by looking at the teachings he imparted to these two brothers.

At that time northwest India was dominated by Muslim rule, and Muslim kings had begun to invade south India. It was a period of social, cultural, religious, and spiritual upheaval. Vidyaranya inspired kings Harihara and Bukka to organize their strength to defend righteousness, and under his guidance these two brothers, sons of an ordinary local king, became the powerful rulers of the empire called Bijaya Nagaram. Nowhere else in history do we find two kings ruling the same territory peacefully. Yet these brothers, because of the high spiritual training they had received from their master, were able to rule together. And the fact that south India surpasses the north in cultural richness can be credited to the influence of Vidyaranya Yati and his two emperor disciples.

Vidyaranya continued his spiritual practices meticulously for decades, but deep down he felt empty and lonely. He knew that there is a vast difference between knowing the truth intellectually and experiencing it directly, and he longed for the direct experience. So at the age of fifty-four he left his career of teacher and writer, one that had brought him fame and wealth, and feeling the need for personal guidance from a *sadguru* (spiritual master), he was initiated into the order of Shankaracharya by a great and learned saint, Shankarananda. At that time he was given the name Swami Vidyaranya Yati.

Now Vidyaranya focused his energy on *shravana* (study), *manana* (contemplation), and *nididhyasana* (the practical application of the Vedantic teachings). He also continued his intense practice of meditation on the *gayatri* mantra. And just as he had in his early youth and adulthood, Vidyaranya gained fame and honor as a renunciate. He was believed to have the highest spiritual attainment in the country, but he openly acknowledged his frustration at his lack of spiritual experience. His followers and admirers thought he was being humble, but Vidyaranya knew the depth of his own imperfection. He worked hard to deepen his practice; prayers flowed from his heart incessantly, but nothing seemed to work, even though his desire to attain enlightenment was intense. He began to wonder if the problems lay with him or with the practice. Utterly dejected, he quietly left the monastery.

By this time Vidyaranya was an old man. His body had already become a burden, and his mind was even heavier. He was not sure of where to go and what to do, but one thing was certain: he had no interest in the world anymore.

One day as he passed through a lonely cremation ground he saw a man walking toward him who, despite his rough appearance, seemed to be completely at peace. "May I have the honor to greet you, sir?" the man said. "It will be my honor to have you as my guest, even for a few moments."

"Why not?" Vidyaranya replied. "I have nothing else to do."

The man exclaimed, "What seems to be the trouble, O learned teacher?"

"It doesn't matter," Vidyaranya answered. "Who are you and what do you do here at the cremation ground? What makes you so peaceful and cheerful in a place like this?"

As he spoke, Vidyaranya suddenly noticed a magnificent pavilion (unheard of at a cremation ground) and people spreading carpets on a platform. He couldn't believe his eyes. "Who are you?" he asked the stranger. "Are you a magician? How did you materialize all this?"

"I am an adept of the mysterious spiritual path called *aghora marga*," the man responded. "I am a resident of these charnel grounds. Destruction is creation for me. External ugliness enhances my internal beauty. I embrace the things that have been discarded by all. What you see here, or anywhere else in the world, is *lila*, the divine game of the great Lord Bhairava, who simultaneously creates, maintains, and destroys the manifest world. I am That. You are That."

Bewildered, Vidyaranya pleaded, "Forgive me, sir, if because of my ignorance I appeared to be disrespectful. My only question is: What is wrong with me that I have been practicing my best for more than eighty years but have gained no direct experience of this truth?"

"Your previous *samskaras* have not been fully destroyed," the sage answered. "That is why you have not been able to have the fruit of your practice."

"But why is it taking so much time to overcome my previous karmas?" Vidyaranya argued. "According to the scriptures, the task of overcoming past karma can be accomplished by doing just one *maha purashcharana* of the *gayatri* mantra. I have done it not just once but several times."

The sage responded, "Because you were born a brahmin in a scholarly and priestly family, you learned this mantra from a book and began practicing it as a custom. Early on you became a teacher, but you never got a chance to be a student. Therefore things are going slowly for you. Look behind you."

Vidyaranya turned and saw six fires that had been extinguished. A seventh, in the distance, was still burning. "These represent your seven past lives," the sage continued. "Karmas corresponding to six lifetimes have been reduced to ashes. But the *gayatri shakti* [the power of the gayatri mantra] has not yet consumed all the karma from your past. That is why the seventh pile is still burning. Have patience."

"How much patience, sir," Vidyaranya pleaded, "and for how long? Have pity on me! Help me achieve the goal of my life before this body is dropped off."

"That is not in conformity with the divine will," the sage replied. "Don't push yourself beyond what you can sustain. Continue to do your practice, and in the natural course of time you will attain the final result."

Vidyaranya realized that he had found his *sadguru* and begged for initiation—not the ordinary initiation, but rather *shaktipata*. The sage told him it was too soon, but Vidyaranya insisted.

The sage finally relented. He recited the gayatri mantra to

Vidyaranya and then told him to sit down and repeat it. When he did so the Divine Mother, the Goddess Gayatri, appeared before him in all her brilliance and glory. At first glance Vidyaranya was overwhelmed and delighted, but his joy quickly turned to anger. "What kind of mother are you that you ignore your child and come to his rescue only when he is old?" he cried. "You merciless, stone-hearted mother! May you turn into stone and stay at this cremation ground!"

As Vidyaranya completed his sentence, the Divine Mother turned into a statue, and instantly Vidyaranya realized what a mistake he had made. Crying for mercy, he fell at the feet of his master. "I told you to have patience," the sage responded, "and not make undue demands—but it is all right. This was destined to happen. Now stay here. Offer your worship to her, and in your remaining life try to assimilate the mystery that underlies as well as transcends both duality and non-duality."

How long Vidyaranya lived after this experience and where he dropped his body no one knows. Tradition tells us that he lived a long life, one that probably exceeded a hundred years, and that his teachings were an inspiration to many. The following questions and answers, which have been taken from Vidyaranya's writings, provide us with a glimpse of these teachings.

S e e k e r : Can truth—Brahman, Atman, the pure Self— be known by logic and reasoning, or is it known directly through intuitive revelation, or through a combination of both?

V i d y a r a n y a : The actual experience of pure Self comes from "Self-revelation." The truth reveals itself to the knower, and when this happens the knower becomes a *rishi* [a seer]. It is not that the *rishi* sees the truth but that the truth shows itself to the *rishi,* thus transforming the blessed aspirant into a "seer." Rather than being illuminated by the mind or the intellect, truth dawns.

However, the study of scriptures helps sharpen the intellect and keeps us from becoming complacent about our present level of understanding. Logic and reasoning are a function of the intellect, which is a fine instrument for gaining secondhand knowledge. So you must train your intellect in order to read and understand the maps of spirituality that the sages have drawn, maps that are based on their direct experience.

These maps are called the scriptures, and by following them you can safely and confidently tread the path and one day reach the goal and see directly. This is called revelation. Reasoning can overcome doubt, but if it is not guided properly it can create even more serious doubt and confusion. Therefore let your reasoning be attuned to the revealed scriptures, and whenever you notice a conflict between the two, rely on the scriptures. But even when you do this, you need your intellect to penetrate this intent. In other words, the intellect is a fine tool, but it needs to be used properly.

S e e k e r : What do you mean when you say that the truth alone—Brahman, Atman, the Self—is real and the world is illusory?

V i d y a r a n y a : The world is illusory in the sense that everything in the external world is constantly changing. Objects of the world are transitory—subject to death, decay, and destruction. But in spite of knowing this, we fail to remember that the objects we presently have in hand are subject to this same law. All objects suffer the same fate, whether we believe it or not. Lack of this knowledge results in disappointment.

All worldly relationships follow the same law. When we are young we think we will never become old, even though we see those around us age. When our own old age approaches, we are disappointed and afraid. We try to escape this by using herbs, medicines, cosmetics, or just by keeping ourselves busy. But nothing helps. That which you think you are is constantly slipping through your fingers.

In your relationships with others the situation is even worse. Those who seem to love you today don't care for you tomorrow. Your children tell you they love you, but eventually they marry and devote themselves to their own children. You are left alone with your own false sense of I-am-ness, which is constantly in flux. It is in this sense that the scriptures say the world is illusory—not to dishearten you or make you sad, but so you can accept it as a fact and overcome your disappointments.

While you are trying to assimilate this knowledge of the illusory nature of worldly objects, contemplate on the truth that is immortal and not subject to death, decay, and destruction. This truth remains unchanged while it witnesses the changing states of worldly objects, including your own body and mind. Once you know that eternal truth, then life's successes and failures, its losses and gains, will no longer disappoint you. Instead of seeing destruction beneath this stream of change, you will see "newness," and this experience will be different from anything you have ever known before. You will appreciate the process of change, for you will understand that without it, the world would become stale and stagnant and eventually decay.

S e e k e r : Once you know this truth directly from within, then are you really free from the bondage of birth and death? Do you become immortal, as the scriptures say?

V i d y a r a n y a : Of course. A knower of the eternal Self becomes immortal. But this does not mean that you will never die: it means that you transcend your attachment to worldly objects, including your own body; it means that you will be able to maintain the joy of simply being. The body is composed of different elements and so it must decompose one day. Death is merely a habit of the body.

While we are alive we are motivated by our desire to undertake certain actions. In most cases they are goal-oriented. If we fail to achieve the fruits of our actions, we are disappointed and depressed; if we succeed, we become attached. And this attachment leads to fear, because sooner or later we lose what we have gained—the objects we worked so hard for are destroyed before we depart, or we must eventually leave them.

Desire itself is never destroyed, however. It is desire that forces us to perform our actions—which keep creating misery—and we keep performing more actions that we think will make us happy. And because many desires are not fulfilled in this lifetime, those that are unfulfilled create the psychological conditions that lead to the cycles of birth and death.

To free yourself from these cycles you must cultivate an attitude of non-attachment toward worldly objects. And that comes only when you know that there is a higher truth. Only then will you not be tempted by the charms and temptations of the world. Then, after knowing the higher truth *[para vidya]*, the lower truth *[apara vidya]* loses its binding power. In the light of higher truth, lower truth becomes illusory. An enlightened person knows that the external world is like water in a mirage. It is a waste of time to run after it—it cannot quench your thirst. Ignore such appearances and seek the oasis of peace and happiness: Brahman, the highest truth.

S e e k e r : I have heard that after knowing Brahman, you really do experience oneness with Brahman. Is this true?

V i d y a r a n y a : Whatever you know, you believe in, and for you that is the only reality. Your concepts of pleasure and pain, loss and gain, bondage and freedom remain confined to the objects in your field of knowing. In this tiny, illusory world you fashion your self-image: you find yourself poorer than someone else, richer than someone else, and so forth. And because of your limited vision of the truth you remain a victim of numberless self-created complexes.

Thus if you identify yourself as a merchant, you derive delight from getting richer than other merchants, and you conceptualize heaven as a place where you can enjoy the riches you couldn't attain on Earth. For those who live in the desert, heaven is filled with oases, and hell has no water. In other words, such concepts of heaven and hell, bondage and freedom correspond to your self-image, which is a reflection of the circumstances of your little world. In this little world, you either love your self-image or you hate it. But whatever the case, you are afraid of losing it because you believe it is the dearest thing you have. Those with superiority or inferiority complexes either appreciate or depreciate themselves, but in the final analysis they do not want to lose what they are.

Nevertheless, as circumstances change, our self-image changes and falls apart in spite of all our efforts to sustain it. We can't stop this process of change. It makes us insecure and fearful—it becomes a continuous death that we experience before the actual death of the body. Thus the knower of the lower reality remains in the lower reality.

You are whatever you know yourself to be. This is a simple law. *"Bramavit Brahmaiva bhavati"*: The knower of Brahman becomes Brahman. The moment you know that you are inseparable from universal consciousness, you become that universal consciousness. Your faith in that consciousness will grow and your self-image will be transformed. You will no longer feel better or worse than anyone else. You will become free from all complexes, for in you all complexes and diversities find their rightful place and become an integral part of you. Their diverse and seemingly contradictory appearances beautify your unified awareness. You understand that you are not "part of collective consciousness": you *are* collective consciousness.

Changes that take place within the realm of consciousness do not affect the eternity of consciousness. For example, in a forest there are plants, shrubs, vines, animals, insects, rocks, and so forth. If we look at everything that exists in that forest individually, we will not see the forest as such, although we can't deny the existence of the forest. From the standpoint of an individual tree in the forest, the passing of a particular plant or insect may be sad to you, but from the perspective of the forest it is all part of growth. Even if the entire forest were to catch on fire, it would still exist because the potential for regeneration would be there. The forest as such never dies when its individual entities are destroyed.

Once you identify yourself with universal consciousness, you experience oneness with everything and find delight in witnessing changes taking place in the external world as well as in yourself. Your fear of death, decay, and destruction vanishes; you become

119

fearless. And because of this, you love all and reject none, for you know that everyone and everything in the universe is simply an elaboration of yourself. In this state of realization, love is your spontaneous expression because that has become your nature.

S e e k e r : If Atman—the Self, pure consciousness—is the only eternal reality and is not subject to birth and death or bondage and freedom, then why do we need to do *sadhana*? Who does the practice and who receives its fruit?

V i d y a r a n y a : Atman is pure and enlightened, subject to neither birth nor death, and therefore it does not require freedom from bondage. It is never bound by any law. It is the mind that ignorantly believes itself to be in bondage and strives for liberation. Spiritual practices are meant to liberate the mind, not Atman. Mind, with all its employees—the senses and the body—does the practice, and if it is lucky it gets the reward. Atman, the pure Self, stands still from eternity to eternity and witnesses the play performed by this master magician called mind.

Once mind creates the concept of bondage and is convinced that it is bound, it cannot rest until it is again convinced that it is totally free. But its conviction of bondage is so strong that it must go through an arduous untying of its restraints. That is called *sadhana*.

S e e k e r : Why do we need to do any practice? Why not just study, contemplate, and gain the conviction that we are That and then become That?

V i d y a r a n y a : Through study and contemplation on the truth as described in the *Vedas*, you transcend a false identification with the non-self, which is destroyed by knowledge of your true Self, and you experience yourself as a pure, unalloyed, totally independent wave of consciousness—Atman. You achieve this much by virtue of your contemplative knowledge. But you are not a perfectly free being until you have achieved the unlimited grandeur, knowledge, and bliss within, which can be brought forward only by awakening and unfolding the infinite power of Brahman. This comes about through sadhana.

It is as if you were a billionaire who has completely forgotten about the money he has in the bank. If he remembers, he is no longer poor, he is a billionaire! But finding his passbook, getting out the money, and spending it the way he wants is an entirely different thing. That you do through sadhana. You won't be able to claim your wealth if you don't know it exists. For that purpose you need strong, convincing knowledge—your passbook.

The scriptures in which the sages confirm the existence of Atman and its infinite power—*atma shakti*—are that passbook. Your unshakable conviction, fully supported by reason and logic, is like reading your name on the passbook and realizing what the balance is. On the ground of this realization grows the desire to find the source of your wealth, and acquainting yourself with the routes to that destination is like learning the proper system of sadhana. Following the best route is like seeking direct guidance from a teacher. And finally, reaching the source of your wealth and attaining that which was already yours is called the realization not only of who you are, but also of how great you are and how infinite.

During his long life Vidyaranya wrote several immortal works, including a commentary on the *Vedas;* the Vedantic texts *Panchadashi* and *Jivan-Mukti-Viveka;* and an encyclopedic tantric text on *Sri Vidya* titled *Shrividyarnava*. In these texts he explains profound philosophical theories and addresses the pressing spiritual and philosophical issues that we face in our day-to-day life.

MADHUSUDANA SARASVATI

*M*adhusudana Sarasvati was born at the beginning of the sixteenth century and rose to fame as a brilliant philosopher. It was
a time of rapid and multifaceted scholastic development in India,
and scholars were writing prolific commentaries on the scriptures as
well as independent treatises from various philosophical perspec-
tives. Powerful commentators—such as Ramanuja, Vallabha,
Madhva, Nimbarka—and a host of their followers produced a huge
body of such literature, using the *Upanishads,* the *Brahma Sutra,* and
the *Bhagavad Gita* to support their position. They often embraced
a dualistic worldview.

In response, monks and scholars from the Shankaracharya tradition rushed to defend their own non-dualistic viewpoint, and in
the process of attempting to establish the superiority of advaita over
all other philosophical systems, they turned advaita into a dry intellectual game. In many cases its practical aspects were lost and only
intellectual gymnastics remained. As a result, advaita failed to illu-
minate the hearts of spiritual seekers.

Madhusudana was such a scholar. He belonged to the school
that used logical, arid reasoning as a powerful tool for tearing apart

other philosophical systems. His *Advaita Siddhi,* which emphatically proves the existence of non-dual, absolute truth, refutes almost all existing philosophical tenets and reduces them to the point at which they seem illogical and meaningless. *Advaita Siddhi* leaves no space for any principle other than pure, objective knowledge. Intellect is its ground; logic is its force; and understanding non-dual truth is its goal.

Deep down, however, Madhusudana was a spiritual seeker more than he was a philosopher. He adhered to Shankaracharya's non-dualistic philosophy, but he was at heart an independent thinker. And as he continued to study, teach, write, and contemplate the truth that he preached, he realized that he was still empty. He recalled the memories of his childhood and the pure and simple spiritual practices he had been exposed to in those days. He remembered how much he had loved Lord Krishna, and how sweet it had been to see his parents and other family members worshipping Him. Now that he was an adult, he saw many sages who, though not as educated as he, seemed to be happier and more spiritually evolved.

Madhusudana pushed his intellect aside, and the devotional part of his being came forward. Soon he fell in love with Lord Krishna again. But he continued to teach the philosophy of non-dualism in public. He began to lead a double life. In the presence of his students and followers he was a staunch non-dualistic philosopher, but in his private life he was a devotee of the Lord. Publicly he was busy lecturing and writing on the absolute non-dual Brahman, but secretly he worshipped Lord Krishna and prayed that one day he would have a direct vision of Him. As time passed, this grew into a burning desire for communion, and he cut down on his lecturing and writing to spend more time meditating on the beautiful form of his *ishta devata* (chosen deity).

Years passed. Madhusudana's sadhana gradually became more intense, and finally he moved to Brindavan, the birthplace of Lord Krishna. But there His devotees carried on as if they were drunk on divine love: they smeared themselves with the dust of the land which long ago had touched the lotus feet of the Lord; like madmen, they embraced the plants and shrubs as though they were embracing the Lord incarnate. Madhusudana tried to create this devotional mood by doing what the others did, but he did not feel the slightest touch of the ecstasy they seemed to be experiencing.

He would approach the devotees, prostrate at their feet, beg for their mercy and grace, and seek their blessing so that one day he too could see the Lord. One would say to him, "Rub the dust of this land all over your body and tune your mind and heart to the songs of the birds who are constantly singing the praises of the Lord. Through the specks of dust you will feel His touch. In the songs of the birds you will hear His name." Madhusudana tried, but it didn't work. Others would say, "Go to the River Yamuna and take a dip in the water that resembles the blue complexion of the Lord. Ask the river whether she has seen the Lord recently, sporting with His playmates on her bank. Ask the kadamba tree whether it has seen the Lord sitting somewhere on its branch. Open your eyes, O Madhusudana. This land is pervaded by the Lord. Purify yourself in the holy land of Brindavan. You will see Him, hear Him, smell Him, and touch Him." Still others would say, "Open your heart and wait for the Lord to come in. Break down the doors made of your intellectual knowledge and you will instantly see that He is more eagerly awaiting you than you are Him."

All this made very little sense to Madhusudana. Then one night he dreamed that a voice told him to go to the holy city of Banaras, and there he would receive proper initiation in the path of divine love directly from a master. Only then, he dreamed, would he attain a glimpse of the Lord. Madhusudana set out at once.

Soon after he arrived in Banaras a mysterious saint approached Madhusudana and offered him guidance. "I am Bhairava," he said, "the destroyer of the world that stands on the ground of illusion." A beautifully mysterious and profound conversation ensued. What follows is a fragment from that dialogue.

M a d h u s u d a n a : Why is it that even though I am constantly searching for the Lord, He has not yet given me His *darshana* [a glimpse of His real presence]?

B h a i r a v a : In your case, your philosophy is the barrier between you and the Lord. There is a conflict between it and actual practice. Philosophically, you are feeding your intellect with the idea of the absolute non-dual Brahman which transcends all names and forms. You tell yourself that absolute truth is without any qualities and characteristics, that it is completely different from this manifest world and from any kind of personal God you may have conceptualized. This philosophy itself undermines the impact of your sadhana, which inclines you to have a direct experience of a God who is not transcendent, but immanent.

The Lord Krishna that comes to your mind has a form and a name and is endowed with certain qualities and characteristics. He is someone you can talk to. He is tangible, perceivable. A God with these qualities does not fit the Brahman of your philosophy. And because you have never acknowledged this conflict you have made your spiritual life a battlefield, and you are fighting on both sides. For a few hours a day you want your Brahman, the absolute reality, to supersede Krishna. And for the next few hours you want Lord Krishna to play His flute for you. How is this possible? You are in limbo.

M a d h u s u d a n a : How can I overcome this conflict, Master?

B h a i r a v a : You are not innocent, Madhusudana, and that is why it is hard for you. You are a powerful intellectual, but you have also nurtured your devotional virtues to a high degree. Meditation, contemplation, prayer, and other yogic techniques will not allow your devotion to conquer your intellect easily, nor vice versa.

M a d h u s u d a n a : Am I a hopeless case?

B h a i r a v a : Not at all. You have already received the grace of the Lord; that is how you got here. You need only the final touch and you will be there. Now go back to Brindavan and continue your sadhana. That land, which the scriptures call Goloka Dhama, is a connecting link between this world and the subtle realm of the Lord. In that eternal world He sports with His *shaktis,* and blessed souls enjoy their company.

Just as the darkness of the night is dispelled by dawn, the vision of the Lord will dispel your intellectual confusion and emotional instability. You will be free from conflict, and the next moment you will see the rising sun—the Lord in His full brilliance and glory. May that mystery be unveiled to you.

With his master's blessings, Madhusudana returned to the land of Brindavan and engaged in intense sadhana according to the sage's instructions. And as the day of his enlightenment neared, his heart was filled with increasingly intense love and longing for the Lord. His intellect began to lose the power to chase away the force of his devotion. The maya he had previously thought to be negative and binding he now saw as the divine consort of Brahman. The Brahman that had previously seemed inactive, passive, and almost inanimate was now vibrant as it pulsated internally with intrinsic ripples of bliss and beauty.

This experience was incomprehensible, and yet Madhusudana felt it. He was overwhelmed. And not knowing what to think, he simply surrendered himself to it and prayed to the Lord to give him the strength to understand and appreciate what he was undergoing. Then, as the moment of the actual vision approached, Madhusudana was transported into a state of trance, and in this state he was totally one with the Lord. He was the Lord.

But that is not what he had been yearning for. He wanted to have a vision of the Lord, and that was possible only if the Lord was separate from him. He wanted a taste of the divine love that a devotee receives from the loving glance of the Lord. And so, still in a trance-like state, he stepped back from this state of oneness and found himself in a state in which he and the Lord were on equal ground. But he was embarrassed to see the Lord and himself on the same platform, so he stepped back again and saw the Lord on a higher platform.

The Lord knew, however, that Madhusudana wanted to see Him in totally manifest form—not just through the eye of the mind but also through his physical eyes. And so, through the power of grace, Madhusudana's mind, which was still absorbed within, was now pulled outward. He became aware of his physical existence, and with that awareness he opened his eyes and saw the Lord standing in front of him.

Once again he went into a trance, though he was still awake. Words rushed forward from the depth of his soul. He knelt with folded hands and these words flowed through him: "I see the beautiful flute in Thy hand. How captivating is the blue aura that emanates from Thy body! How golden are the clothes You are wearing! How can I grasp the redness of Thy lips that are so celestially bright? How illuminating and cooling is Thy countenance, which surpasses the beauty and delight of a million full moons! The only words I find to describe Thine eyes are that they are like lotus blossoms. I do not know any higher truth than my Lord Krishna."

How can anyone describe Madhusudana's internal states as he received this vision if he, himself, could not do so? Nevertheless, the experience enlightened both his mind and heart, and a tremendous transformation spontaneously followed. Knowledge and devotion manifested in him in their perfect brilliance and glory, and from that time on the highest degree of intellectual grasp and devotional ecstasy manifested in his thought, speech, and action. Philosophers and spiritual seekers alike sought his guidance, and even those who did not belong to the Shankaracharya order honored his words as the final authority.

After he attained the vision of the Lord, Madhusudana saw the shortcomings of purely scholarly writings clearly, especially those which strictly advocated the path of knowledge. He understood that knowledge without *bhakti* is like a lake without fresh water—it fails to quench one's thirst. And the powerful transformational philosophy and spiritual teachings that followed are clearly re-flected in his later writings. His commentary on the *Bhagavad Gita,* for example, leads aspirants away from either extreme intellectual-ism or extreme devotionalism and toward the balanced stance of the ancient Vedic sages. This viewpoint can be glimpsed in his an-swer to a question on the nature of God:

S e e k e r : How can God, the highest truth, be transcendent and immanent simultaneously, and thus respond to your love and devotion? According to *advaita bhakti* [the non-dualistic path of love and devotion] one can be inseparable from God and at the same time be different from God. How is this possible?

M a d h u s u d a n a : Absolute truth is not subject to our belief or disbelief. It remains transcendent even if we believe it to be immanent. However, under certain conditions Brahman, the tran-scendental truth, is experienced as immanent even though its transcendence is ever maintained.

Brahman is pure consciousness. It is absolute, transcendent, unchanging, eternal, and always free. But as the stream of life man-ifests from this source, it assumes a form which consists of multiple layers of reality. Some of these are more subtle, invisible, and intan-gible than others, and in these different layers of our being, consciousness flows in various grades and degrees. The existence of transcendental Brahman is experienced differently at each level.

In other words, we identify ourselves variously from level to level. When we are aware of our bodies, we think ourselves to be bodies; when we are aware of the mind, we think ourselves to be mind; and with the awareness of Atman, the individual Self, we feel that we are different from the mind but still separate from other human beings. At each level, we derive different kinds of satisfac-tion from different relationships. The body receives pleasure from physical relationships, the mind from psychological relationships, and the individual Self from a personal relationship with the higher Self. Brahman, however, delights in itself.

For those whose consciousness is confined to the body and external world, the idea of pure, transcendental truth seems to be fiction. For them, God must be tangible, localized, and capable of responding to their needs. So the transcendental God that is one with the Self (Brahman) seeps through to their individual Self (Atman), mind, and brain, and an image of God is sculpted there. This God is never more real or unreal than our own bodies. And just as we cannot expect to secure our mental health if we ignore our physical health, so do we face numberless obstacles on our inward journey if we ignore this personal God. On the other hand, just as the totality of our existence is not confined to the body, and just as our peace and happiness are not confined to physical pleasure, the worship of an external image of God cannot give complete fulfillment.

But sincere seekers can use this kind of God and their relationship with Him as a stepping-stone to the next level of realization. And from that standpoint it is perfectly correct to say that God is immanent and that aspirants who are entirely separate from God require his mercy in order to overcome the present level of pain and misery that forces them to remain caught in body consciousness.

The process of God-realization, however, must go to the next level. At this stage, from the standpoint of Atman or individual consciousness, God is transcendent and immanent simultaneously, and the individual Self is part of God. This realization gives seekers greater solace; they can say, "I am part of God, but how unfortunate that I don't experience it all the time!" Intense longing takes hold of them, and instead of reciting prayers and performing rituals, which they did at the earlier level, they find prayers flooding the mind and heart spontaneously.

These aspirants have still not experienced oneness with the absolute, but they are aware that the devotional relationship is beyond the level of the body. It is a virtue of the heart, a condition of the mind. It needs a focus—an actual, conceivable object to which all thoughts and emotions can be channeled. Now the external God, who had previously dwelt in the temple, rushes to commune with devotees in their heart. God is no longer an external image; God has become an indweller.

This personal relationship with an impersonal God who is infinite fits within the finite vessel of the body-mind. And with this relationship as a support, the limited individual self—feeling that real joy will dawn only when the "part" that he or she is dissolves into the "whole" and becomes whole—tries to merge with the beloved Self (Brahman), who is perfect and universal. The moment that happens, the seeker experiences the oneness of the individual self and the universal Self, and there is no possibility thereafter of one loving the other—because there is only One.

The first two stages of this process are called the process of *bhakti*. Just as it is the nature of the ocean to express itself as waves, at this stage waves of love continually appear and subside from the ocean of unitary love. The last stage of experiencing oneness is simply the state of bhakti, which is all that remains. This is pure love. Only in this state, the state of absolute samadhi, do blessed devotees experience pure love without movement. When they come back to outward consciousness, they enjoy vibrant love. In the scriptures the pure state of love is called *para bhakti*—the highest form of bhakti—while the first two levels are called *apara bhakti,* the lower form of bhakti. They are each valid in their rightful place and stage. This is the indescribable mystery of the transcendent reality.

SWAMI RAMA OF THE HIMALAYAS

Swami Rama is the contemporary link in the long lineage of Himalayan sages. His non-dualistic philosophy stems from the *Vedas* and *Upanishads*. A yogi, philosopher, and scientist, he brought science and spirituality together to create a bridge between East and West, between Indian philosophy and Western psychology. And without disturbing the religious faith of either East or West, he introduced a practical method of bringing about the spiritual unfoldment and total well-being of everyone regardless of their religion or nationality.

Swami Rama was born in the first quarter of the twentieth century in the Garhwal region of the Himalayas. His father was famous for his knowledge of the scriptures, but late in life he became deeply withdrawn and decided to renounce the world. His family was provided for, so he set out for the shrine known as Chandi Devi, near Haridwar, and there he began an intense sadhana. Six months passed.

One day a tall, thin, radiant yogi visited the shrine who, as it turned out, was an adept of the Himalayas—the famous sage known as Bengali Baba, or Babaji. He stayed with the old man for three days and taught him a systematic method of sadhana, and then he told him to go home. Soon, the sage said, the old man and his wife would be blessed with a child who would follow the path of light.

In due time Swami Rama was born, and a few days later Babaji appeared and asked the new parents to give the infant to him. With a little hesitation, the mother put the child in Babaji's lap. The sage looked at the infant a long time, and then gave him back to his mother, saying, "Take care of him. When the time comes I will be back for him. Remember, he is my child—not yours."

While the boy was still quite young, his father died and Babaji took responsibility for raising him. He saw to it that the boy was educated in established schools and colleges even though formal education was not the favorite part of the boy's young life. The moment school was over, he eagerly returned to his master to pursue his spiritual and yogic training. After early childhood had passed, he began to receive practical lessons in discipline and proper behavior. And because Babaji preferred to live in seclusion in the caves and huts of the high mountains, the boy was exposed to a wide range of spiritual teachers and seekers as he traveled with his master. The sages called him Bhole (innocent boy).

Babaji began Bhole's spiritual training by sending him to one of his disciples, Swami Shivananda, or Gangotri Wale (not to be confused with the Swami Sivananda of the Divine Light Society), in the majestic Gangotri region of the Himalayas. One of his master's most advanced disciples, Swami Shivananda began to teach the boy the scriptures as well as the actual disciplines one needs on the path of spiritual unfoldment.

The training required that the teacher be tough, and there were times when the argumentative and rebellious part of Bhole came forward and he refused to be disciplined. Then Swami Shivananda, usually a man of depthless wisdom, patience, endurance, and tolerance, would send him back to his master. When this happened Babaji would remind Bhole that obstinacy, lack of discipline, and disrespect for the teacher can prevent an aspirant from advancing spiritually. Like a loving parent, he first gave the boy a gentle hint. Then he advised him like a friend. And finally, like a teacher, he told him emphatically to go back to Swami Shivananda and behave properly. In this way Bhole passed his early years.

By the time he reached his preteen years, Bhole had adjusted to a monastic, ascetic life. But those who enter spiritual life come from the world, and carry samskaras which must be removed. So when Bhole became a teenager, his master guided him in undertaking powerful spiritual disciplines to burn even the subtlest seeds of previous samskaras.

To this end, Babaji brought Bhole to the holy city of Banaras and arranged to have a small hut built across the river from the city, facing the Ganga. A small thatched roof extended over the door, and he drew a line charged with a protective spiritual energy *(lakshmana rekha)* around the hut and instructed Bhole not to cross it except to perform his morning and evening ablutions. He then initiated Bhole in *gayatri purashcharana,* a long and specific course of meditation to be taken while he lived in solitude, and told him not to pay attention to anything or anyone outside the line until the practice was complete. "No matter what goes on outside the line," he said, "pay attention to your practice and be aware of your goal the whole time."

Babaji then lit a *dhuni* (fire) for Bhole under the overhang just outside the door. It was to be his only friend, night and day. A pandit from the city, who was also a disciple of Babaji, was assigned to provide food once a day, and Bhole was told to complete 2,400,000 repetitions of the gayatri mantra in sixteen months.

He began the practice. A few months passed, and people from the city came to know about this young, vibrant *brahmachari* (apprentice swami) and began to visit him, impressed by how calm and tranquil he was, and at the same time how vibrant and energetic. The less attention Bhole paid to visitors, the more impressed they were.

But there was also a group of hecklers who came to visit Bhole, determined to disturb him. And one day, when he had been doing

135

his practice for eleven months, they challenged him to a debate. Bhole remained silent, but they persisted. Finally he lost his temper, crossed the boundary line, caught hold of someone's neck, and pushed him toward the Ganga. The hecklers dispersed, but soon afterward the pandit who was supplying him with food appeared and handed him a telegram from his master. It read: "You have ruined your practice. Start over."

With a strong resolve not to commit such a mistake again, Bhole began once more. Again, almost a year passed. The time for testing had arrived, and one night, around midnight, a dwarf came to the hut and sat in front of the fire, keeping outside the boundary line so there was a good distance between himself and Bhole. Neither broke the silence. The dwarf stayed almost two hours. The next night he came again at exactly the same time and sat there in silence, just as he had the night before. Night after night, the dwarf visited Bhole without disturbing him.

Then one night the dwarf brought Bhole a gift of *jalebi* (Indian sweets) and milk. The young renunciate was delighted, and from then on the dwarf brought jalebi and milk every night. Bhole began to wonder, however, how the dwarf managed to get across the river in the middle of the night when there were no boats, and where the dwarf found the jalebi when the shops were closed. So one night he asked him outright who he was, how he got there, and where he got the sweets.

The dwarf replied, "You are doing your job and I am doing mine. I never disturb you. By serving you I do my work the way I am instructed to." He refused to say more.

Enraged, Bhole poured a few drops of water on his right palm and raised his hand to the dwarf, shouting, "Tell me who you are or I'll destroy you!" The dwarf did not move. Once again Bhole demanded to know who he was. Still the dwarf remained silent, and finally Bhole lost control of himself. Repeating the gayatri mantra mentally, he threw the water on the dwarf—who vanished instantly! In the spot where he had been sitting there was only a bone.

Bhole knew that he had made a mistake once again—and sure enough, the next day the pandit came with another telegram from Babaji: "You have ruined your practice again. Be strong and conquer these negative and destructive tendencies. Bless you."

Bhole began the practice a third time. And now, through the grace of his master, he completed it. Recounting this story years later, Swami Rama said, "Destructive tendencies keep coming up until they are completely conquered. It's not easy to do this, but neither is it impossible. Blessed are those who make a sincere effort to work with themselves at every level."

Babaji now made Bhole travel in the mountains, from cave to cave and monastery to monastery, visiting the adepts of all traditions. Babaji wanted him to gain a wide range of experiences, and the lessons Bhole got from these masters added fuel to his desire to know the truth at every level.

During these travels Bhole's desire to attain the highest state of Self-realization became even more intense. He repeatedly asked Babaji to initiate him in *sannyasa* (the path of renunciation), but his master kept avoiding the request, insisting that he should renounce the world only after he had come to understand it thoroughly.

Many years later Swami Rama remembered his master's advice: "My son, in order to connect and establish yourself completely 'there,' you must first free yourself from the fetters 'here.' The greater part of sadhana consists of crossing the mire of illusion. That is where the effort is needed. The knowledge of the truth is self-evident. It is a matter of revelation which occurs instantly and spontaneously. But unless you are completely fed up with the deceptive nature of this world, worldly people, and worldly activities, you will not have an unwavering, one-pointed commitment to attaining the highest goal. Therefore look closely at this world, especially at the things that appear to be glamorous and those that seem indispensable to your survival. Look also at those who claim to love you, those who are famous, and those who appear to be virtuous and powerful. Do not search for faults in others, but sharpen your

intellect and gain maturity so that you do not become trapped in
this world."

Following these instructions, Bhole traveled widely throughout
India, visiting rich and poor, educated and illiterate, social reformers and businessmen, religious leaders and politicians. He encountered intellectuals and great saints, adept yogis, and preachers.
Sometimes people admired him, and at other times they ridiculed
and condemned him. At times he mistook a magician for an accomplished saint. Once he mistook an adept in deep samadhi for
someone who had fallen asleep. These experiences helped him become sharp in the worldly sense and wise in the spiritual sense.

After several years Bhole had gained knowledge of the world.
He was ready to be initiated as a *sannyasin* (renunciate) and was ordained as a *dandi* swami, the highest order of *sannyasa,* which is
symbolized by a *danda* (a staff that a swami of this order carries all
the time). And along with the danda come strict spiritual disciplines and observances. Babaji blessed Bhole and told him that he
was now free to create his own destiny, that all his previous karmic
bonds had been burned.

Shortly after this, Swami Rama visited his grandmaster in
Tibet and witnessed *parakaya pravesha* (casting off the body volun-
tarily), and learned the esoteric sciences such as *surya vijñana* and
Sri Vidya, all of which he talks about in his book *Living with the
Himalayan Masters.*

When Swami Rama returned from Tibet in 1948, his master
told him to go to the banks of the Narmada River, well away from
human settlements, to intensify his practice. This time, except for a
few villagers who brought him the bare necessities, he was in complete solitude and able to do his sadhana without attracting notice.

But one day a group of hunters arrived at the riverbank and
saw the young *sadhu* sitting quietly with his eyes closed—
surrounded by crocodiles. Neither the man nor the crocodiles showed
any fear. Amazed, the hunters took a few pictures and departed.

The next day the photos were in the newspapers in nearby towns, and people began searching for the young swami. Not many were successful, but those who were spread the story further. Eventually it reached the ears of Dr. Kurtkoti, the Shankaracharya of Karvirpitham, a highly respected and learned scholar and social reformer. Hoping to retire, he had been searching for a successor who could meet all the requirements for holding this spiritual seat, and the young monk who had accidentally been exposed to the camera interested him. So he appointed a group of pandits to visit him and find out how he lived, what he did, and what daily routine he followed.

139

Their reports were favorable, so when Dr. Kurtkoti had gathered as much information as he could, he approached Swami Rama himself and eventually proposed that he accept the position of Shankaracharya. The young swami replied that he would do so only with the permission of his master, who granted it. So in 1949 he was installed in the seat of Shankaracharya of Karvirpitham and was then known by the name of Sadashiva Bharati.

Swami Rama did not know what he was stepping into. Before becoming Shankaracharya, he had lived with Mahatma Gandhi, Rabindranath Tagore, and Sri Aurobindo, all of whom were powerful freethinkers, social reformers, and political leaders. These experiences, as well as his travels throughout the country, had helped him to develop a broad understanding of the social, cultural, and economic aspects of Indian society. And his concept of religion and spirituality was also wider than that of the typical Indian swami.

As Shankaracharya, Swami Rama had the power to help reform Hindu society, and he took an active part in the work of social reform that Dr. Kurtkoti had begun. One of the most important of these projects was a campaign to educate oppressed members of Indian society (including the untouchables) and bring every man and woman into the mainstream, giving them the right to enter temples and worship God just as members of the so-called upper class did.

Swami Rama brought these injustices to the attention of politicians and members of the upper class, but his greatest challenge came from the orthodox brahmins, to whom the concept of change was anathema. Only after a long struggle did he succeed in making reforms.

When he spoke of this time years later, Swami Rama said he left the post of Shankaracharya when he realized how difficult it was to do selfless service and yet enjoy peace of mind. He missed his solitude, his peaceful nights, his most beloved master. He realized that in order for an ashram to be truly spiritual, people first must be taught to distinguish spirituality from religious beliefs, customs, dogmas, and superstitions. Indian society, he found, was not yet ready to embrace the higher values of spirituality, and he knew it was a waste of time to work with those who were not prepared. It was time for him to return to the Himalayas, and one day he slipped quietly away.

Once reunited with his master, this chapter in his life was closed. But out in the world, people continued to search for him. When they found no trace, several hypotheses arose: he was no longer alive; he was hiding somewhere; he had gone abroad; or he was totally absorbed in intense practices somewhere deep in the interior of the forests or the mountains.

This last theory was closest to the truth. Only a few know about this period of Swami Rama's life, which was dedicated to intense sadhana. He later said that these were the best years of his life. He traveled with his master to remote places known only to the *hansas* (the adepts living in the high mountains). He enjoyed the exclusive company of the Himalayas and the Himalayan adepts. Old *sadhus* still remember when he lived in remote places such as Gangotri, Tarkeshwar, and Uttarkashi—holy shrines that lie in the deep recesses of the mountains. With no belongings, not even a water pot, he lived as an *avadhuta,* a *sadhu* who maintains a practice of extreme *aparigraha* (non-possessiveness). After leaving the mountains he spent time in the forests in the Satna district of Madhya Pradesh, Chitrakut, and Vindhyachal in central India.

After several years as an ascetic, Swami Rama returned to the foothills and plains, staying mainly in Allahabad, Kanpur, and Rishikesh. He began to teach and lecture to increasingly large crowds, and always emphasized the importance of creating a bridge between ancient wisdom and the modern sciences, between spirituality and materialism. But underlying everything was the message of the ancient Himalayan sages. The philosophical aspects of what Swami Rama taught were derived from the *Vedas* and *Upanishads;* the principles of holistic health and the body-mind connection he taught were derived from ayurveda, the *Yoga Sutra,* and tantric texts.

Then, after several years, Babaji once again instructed Swami Rama to undergo an intense meditation practice, this time in a cave in the Himalayas, where he was to live for eleven months without seeing a single human being. The entrance of the cave would be closed, but there was an outlet in the back for waste to wash away, and a tiny hole in the ceiling of the cave admitted a single beam of light. During those eleven months he ate a small amount of food once a day—barley and mountain vegetables, some juices, and a glass of milk. He practiced hatha yoga and *pranayama* regularly and slept only two or three hours each day. The rest of the time he meditated. The shaft of light was meant to help concentrate the mind on a single point, and in such a strict environment, either one learns to meditate deeply or one becomes imbalanced and quits.

When he had completed the practice, Swami Rama came out of the cave, and the world looked entirely different. It took him several weeks to reorient himself. In the process, he said later, "I realized that the world was a theater in which one could test one's inner strength, speech, emotions, thoughts, and behavior."

Soon after he completed this practice in the cave, Swami Rama's master told him it was time to go to the West: "You have a mission to complete and a message to deliver," he said. "That message is ours, and you are my instrument."

Swami Rama's first stop on his trip to the West was a brief stay in Japan, where he shared his master's message with Okadasan, the spiritual head of the Mahikari organization. Thus thousands of members came to know him, and in the evenings they arrived by the hundreds to receive his blessing. But after six months it was time to continue his journey.

Before Swami Rama left India, Babaji had told him that he would meet his students and associates in the United States, and that is where he would complete his mission of creating a bridge between East and West. He arrived in the U.S. in 1969, and just as his master had promised, a highly educated core of students soon collected around him. Swami Rama felt that all spiritual practices should be verified scientifically if science has the capacity to do so. And a close interaction with scientists, medical doctors, and psychologists began when he was invited to the Menninger Foundation in Topeka, Kansas, to participate in their research on the mind-body relationship and the mind's capacity to regulate physiological processes, including those thought to be involuntary. By demonstrating his yogic powers, Swami Rama excited the curiosity of scientists and opened new dimensions in the field of parapsychology. But his mission was not confined to any one limited field of learning. His ultimate goal was to introduce the West to the path of spirituality and total health which had been discovered by the ancient sages.

Within a year, Swami Rama founded the Himalayan International Institute of Yoga Science and Philosophy, where he taught a system of holistic living based on the philosophy and practices of yoga and Vedanta. His approach to spirituality in modern times is unique in that it is not affected by religious dogma and cultural bias, it is scientifically verifiable, and it is equally useful to everyone regardless of whether they live in the East or in the West.

Swami Rama always kept his master's words in mind as he transmitted them to his students: People living in both the East and the West have the same purpose in life, although their approaches differ; inner strength, cheerfulness, and selfless service are the basic principles of life everywhere; a human being should be a human being first; a real human being is a member of the cosmos; geographical boundaries have no power to divide humanity. The following material has been gleaned from Swamiji's writings, lectures, and private conversations with his students.

S e e k e r : What is the purpose of life?

S w a m i   R a m a : The purpose of life is to know yourself at every level. The obstacles that may arise from the physical level of your being can be prevented by living in a holistic manner: eating a balanced diet, practicing yogic exercises, regulating the four primitive urges—eating, sleeping, sex, and self-preservation—and going to bed and waking up on schedule.

But after knowing the dynamics of physical well-being and securing it, you come to realize that true happiness does not come from the body: happiness is the creation of the mind. An unhealthy body can create obstacles to achieving peace and happiness, but a healthy body contributes very little to happiness. It is the mind which has to be made healthy, which has to be disciplined and brought under control. Breath is the key to accomplishing this.

A human being is neither body nor mind alone: a human being is also a breathing being. The body and mind are held together with the power of the pranic force, and breath is the major manifestation of that force. As long as people are breathing they are alive, because the breath creates a link between body and mind. The breath works like a customs officer, registering everything that is exported and imported from either side. According to the *Upanishads,* the breath is like a queen bee. The body and mind with all their organs and faculties follow this queen bee.

The degree of health and physical strength you gain by following a holistic lifestyle can be refined and advanced by practicing pranayama. And when seekers are advanced enough to do this, they have the ability to notice subtler causes of disturbance that arise directly from the mind. This is when they must make a commitment to the inward journey—the practice of meditation.

The stream of life is filled with numberless and mysterious currents and crosscurrents, and after making some initial efforts to meditate and noticing a good degree of improvement, students may experience unconscious memories and habit patterns springing up from the depths of the unconscious mind. At this juncture, they cannot escape—nor is there a need to escape—from their own unconscious material, their *samskaras*. Standing on the firm ground of *vairagya*, non-attachment, and with the help of the systematic practice of meditation and contemplation, they can dive deep within, explore the subtle causes of habit patterns, previously unknown to the conscious mind, and return to the safety of that firm ground. In this way they attain freedom from their samskaras once and for all. The mind is free from all conscious and unconscious preoccupations. It is like a clear mirror. And in this mirror, Atman, the inner Self, is reflected spontaneously.

The knowers of truth, those who have completed the entire journey from beginning to end, divide life into three categories: mortal, semi-mortal, and immortal. The body, breath, and conscious mind are the mortal part of the human being. At the other end of the spectrum is the soul, the inner Self, which is immortal. In between is the unconscious mind, which is semi-mortal or semi-immortal. The mortal part of our being goes through the constant change of death, decay, and destruction. It is born, and one day it dies. Whatever actions we perform through this mortal part of ourselves—whether physical, verbal, or mental—create impressions in the unconscious mind. They are stored there in the form of samskaras and motivate our mind, senses, and body to undertake more actions.

This vicious cycle never ends unless we apply the techniques of spiritual discipline. This is because at the time of death, when the body and conscious mind fall apart, human beings are still alive, dwelling in the unconscious mind. And there the samskaras of unfulfilled desires force the unconscious to beg nature to provide them with a new body. And thus human beings go through the process of rebirth.

Once you attain freedom from the samskaras stored in the unconscious, semi-mortal part of your being, however, you realize that you are pure Atman, the eternal Self, which is not subject to either birth or death. Such a realized person is "immortal."

S e e k e r : Then it seems that we must work with the subtle, motivating, powerful seeds that remain dormant in the unconscious mind. How, exactly, do we gain from these samskaras?

S w a m i   R a m a : Discipline is the answer—discipline together with *vairagya*. No matter which path you follow, no matter which practice you undergo, no matter which tradition you belong to, you need a disciplined mind. A confused mind is not fit to follow any path.

Whether you stay at home and pursue your sadhana or renounce your home, you have to face your deep-rooted samskaras. It takes a long time to get rid of them, so do not be disappointed when you find you cannot attain freedom during a month-long retreat. Have patience and keep on working. Cleansing and replacing the contents of your mind is possible when you follow a systematic path of self-discipline.

Stay away from teachers and preachers who profess to teach spirituality and meditation without also teaching discipline. No matter how sound their techniques, unless students are trained to become disciplined it is like sowing seeds in an untilled, barren field. All you really need is to look at the totality of your life, set your priorities, and create a bridge between life within and without. Discipline is the bedrock under that bridge.

S e e k e r : Does one attain the highest goal, Self-realization, through self-effort, God's grace, or a combination of both?

S w a m i   R a m a : In the final analysis, Self-realization happens through God's grace. However, abandoning self-effort, especially in the early stage of the inward journey, is a big mistake. God's grace is like rain that falls over a vast area without any regard for which particular areas will benefit from it. It rains on the unjust and the just alike. Even after it rains, land that is not permeable and cannot hold water, or land that is infertile or without seeds, remains barren. But a fertile land thrives where seeds have been sown and precautions have been taken to make the best use of the rainfall. Plants grow and flowers bloom. So it is with our own preparedness to receive grace, assimilate it, and benefit from it.

In yogic literature, receiving grace is known as receiving *shakti-pata*. And this is possible when a student has gone through a long period of discipline, austerity, and spiritual practice. *Shaktipata* is the natural unfoldment of divine grace. In order to attain the highest realization, however, four types of grace have to converge on one point: *shastra kripa*, the grace of the scriptures; *atma kripa*, the grace of oneself; *guru kripa*, the grace of the guru; and *Ishvara kripa*, the grace of God.

Through *shastra kripa*, the grace of the scriptures, you gain an intellectual understanding of the higher dimensions of life, become inspired, gather courage to follow the path of light, and overcome your trivial concerns and doubts. Then you need *atma kripa*, the grace of your Self, which takes the form of committing yourself to your practice. Sincerity, regularity, staying away from useless things and useless people, and being strong with one's decision is *atma kripa*.

Once you have attained these two graces, you are destined to receive *guru kripa*, the grace of the guru. That is why it is said: "When the student is ready, the guru appears." And once you receive *guru kripa*, which is totally unconditional (from the standpoint of the guru), *Ishvara kripa*, the grace of God, follows automatically. In fact *guru kripa* itself turns into God's grace.

Behind this fourfold grace there is only one functioning force: *karuna*, compassion, the unconditional love of the Divine for all individual souls. It is an internal and ever-flowing stream of divine compassion that manifests in the form of the fourfold grace and leads sincere seekers to the highest goal.

S e e k e r : If I study carefully and do my practices sincerely and faithfully, will I receive guidance directly from within? Or are instructions and guidance from a guru in human form necessary?

S w a m i R a m a : You need an external guru in order to attain the guru within. If you do not have one you may become egotistical, for example, and decide, "I do not need a guru." That is ego talking. Or in your search, if you are not careful, you may become too intellectual and ignore your spontaneous intuition. Or you may become too emotional and ignore your reason. Both situations are equally dangerous. Furthermore, the past several thousand years have produced a vast literature on spirituality, and often novice seekers become confused about which practices they should do and which teachings or practices should be ignored. So you need a guru, a spiritual instructor who has attained realization while following the path that he or she is teaching you.

S e e k e r : They say that it is not easy to find a *sadguru,* a spiritual master. And without a real master, how is it possible to receive true guidance?

S w a m i R a m a : A good student can never meet a bad guru, but the reverse is also true. Similar attracts similar. If for some reason those who are dissimilar meet, the higher force intervenes and drives away those who are not prepared. Do not worry about who is good and who is bad. Increase your capacity. Purify yourself. Acquire the gentle strength within. God will come and say to you, "I want to enter this living temple that you are." Prepare yourself for that situation. Remove the impurities, and you will find that those who want to know reality are themselves the source of reality.

S e e k e r : How do yogis view the phenomenon of death?

S w a m i R a m a : Death is a habit of the body, a necessary change. But while we are alive we don't pay attention to the importance of knowing how to die at will, nor do we prepare ourselves psychologically for that moment. From the moment of birth we constantly tell ourselves that the objects of the world are real and that our happiness and completion depend on material possessions. But there comes a time when we notice that the material objects we have acquired are drastically changing and falling apart, and that the same thing is happening with our relationships. We are disappointed with life, and at the same time we become deeply attached to our children and possessions. As old age approaches we are lonely and afraid. We think that death will be painful—but in fact it is not death, it is the fear of death that creates misery for a dying person.

The brain has a limited capacity to sense physical pain, and at a certain point it becomes oblivious to it. Thus, during death people do not suffer from physical pain as much as they experience psychological pain. So just as we have discovered ways to prepare the expectant mother to have a safe birth and minimize the pain during labor, we must learn the techniques of casting off the body without fear and pain.

Yogis have discovered several ways to cast off their body voluntarily and joyfully. There are many signs and symptoms of impending death, and evolved yogis know precisely when and at what time it will happen. They greet that moment joyfully, and they leave the body in the same way that ordinary human beings take off their clothes.

Some of the famous yogic techniques for casting off the body are *hima-samadhi,* casting off one's body in deep snow; *jala-samadhi,* casting off one's body in water; and *sthala-samadhi,* casting off one's body while sitting in *siddhasana,* the accomplished pose, and consciously opening the fontanelle; meditating on the solar plexus and reducing the body to ashes in a fraction of a second; or by piercing the *brahma randhra,* also known as the *brahma nadi.*

But even if you just meditate regularly and sincerely, you will find that your mantra is an eternal friend during the time of transition. Meditators cannot be lonely and afraid during the time of death, because they are accompanied by the mantra. It is the leader that guides them from this world to the next, and this realization comes a moment before death actually takes place. Thus a dying meditator attains freedom from fear, insecurity, and loneliness in this very lifetime and departs from this platform gracefully.

S e e k e r : I was born and raised in a culture in which I was not exposed to meditation or any form of spiritual discipline, and I do not want to disturb my religious faith. Will this prevent me from advancing on the spiritual path?

S w a m i   R a m a : It doesn't matter where you were born, or which denomination you belong to. As long as you realize the importance of having a healthy body and a balanced mind, you can start practicing those things which make sense to you. You don't have to abandon your faith or embrace another one. Stay wherever you are. Do not disturb your family or your society.

Practice truth in thought, speech, and action. Love for truth will help you understand what your most urgent problems and concerns are. And soon you will notice that you are not interested in either hell or heaven—you simply want to be happy and peaceful.

In the early stages of your inward journey you begin to work with your body, for it is the tool for achieving both worldly and spiritual wealth. You should practice exercises that make your body healthy, whether you are Christian, Hindu, Muslim, Jewish, or Buddhist. Similarly, breathing exercises do not conflict with any religion.

You also need a system of gathering the power of your senses and withdrawing them from the external world. You must learn how to relax and provide maximum rest for your body, senses, and nervous system so that your mind is free from the complaints of your body. This process does not require you to be born in any particular religious or cultural background.

Then comes concentration. At this stage of your inward journey you need to choose an object on which to focus your mind. Make sure that it is intrinsically peaceful and carries the least amount of sectarian baggage. Improve your concentration and one-pointedness by constantly focusing your mind on that one chosen object. By this process you can train your mind to be concentrated.

The mind has a habit of running from one object to another. This roving tendency drains a vast amount of energy and causes weakness and frustration. No one with a scattered mind can expect to be successful either in the external world or in the spiritual world. Practicing a method of concentration makes it possible for you to cultivate one-pointedness. And with the help of a one-pointed mind you can resolve even the most complicated issues. You can penetrate the greatest of all mysteries. You need a purified, one-pointed, and disciplined mind to unveil the truth that saints from different traditions share with us. If you have a healthy body and a one-pointed mind you can practice Christianity, Judaism, Hinduism, Islam, or Buddhism much more accurately and successfully than those who are unhealthy and confused.

According to the sages of the Himalayas the best spiritual discipline is the one that helps you gather the means and resources for undertaking a spiritual practice. That is why they designed a holistic lifestyle, which in ancient times was called *raja yoga*. Simple principles of life—such as practicing non-violence, truthfulness, non-stealing, moderation in sense activity, non-possessiveness, cleanliness, contentment, *tapas* (disciplining the body, mind, and senses), the study of genuine scriptures, and faith in a higher truth—are the foundation of holistic living. There are no religious, ethical, moral, or social schools in the world that do not honor these ten principles.

With the help of this simple practice of spirituality (which consists of these ten principles, plus physical exercise, breathing exercises, relaxation, concentration, and meditation) you automatically begin to overcome your doubt and skepticism. You know what you are doing and you know that it is helping you. You will notice that your understanding of your religious faith, your family life, and your relationships have improved. You have become a more tolerant and loving human being. That is a great achievement in itself.

Afterwards your mind and heart will tell you what should follow next. The process of gradual transformation and unfoldment is
healthy and long-lasting. Depending on your degree of emotional
maturity and intellectual understanding, you will aspire to find a
spiritual path that is perfect for you. There are many jackets in the
market that are attractive and well made, but the best one is one
that fits you. This is also the case with a spiritual path and spiritual
disciplines. All lead to the same goal, but the best path is the one
that suits you. Manmade cultural and religious institutions need to
follow the truth, not the other way around.

THE TEACHINGS IN PERSPECTIVE

It may seem that the teachings of the sages differ from one another, but these differences can be reconciled in one phrase: "The truth is One; its faces are many." In the beginning and intermediate stages of their spiritual unfoldment the sages may have had different experiences, but once they transcended the boundaries of time, space, and causation and reached the highest state of samadhi they all attained the experience of unitary consciousness, the absolute, non-dual Brahman. And as the ultimate truth revealed itself in all its brilliance and perfection, the sages came to know that that which lies outside us also exists within us. With this experience the knowledge of life here and hereafter, the knowledge of manifest and unmanifest reality, was no longer a mystery.

It was impossible, however, for the sages to communicate this experience to those whose consciousness was still confined to apparent reality. The sages had to find a way to bridge the gulf between their realization of unitary consciousness and the consciousness of ordinary people. So they communicated only the part of their experience that was relevant to the specific place and time in which they were teaching. And to do this they employed the language, symbols, and idioms that were in use at that place and time. Thus differences in the teachings are rooted not in differences in the ultimate experience but in how much of that experience the sages were able to share with their students and the idiom in which they communicated it. These differences in presentation aside, however, all sages speak with one voice when describing the way to attain inner unfoldment: "Be practical!"

The sages stress the importance of finding out, at the onset of our journey, where we are in our personal evolution, what our pressing needs are, what our resources are, and how much freedom we have to do what we want to do. They all agree that the only way to minimize obstacles on the journey is to make an accurate assessment of our current situation, and then, once we have done this, to follow a systematic path to reach our goal.

First, we need to look at the broad picture of life. Like an iceberg floating in the ocean of cosmic existence, we see only a small portion of our life at any given time. Like little children, we are happy one moment, cranky the next. We are delighted with trivial matters and at the same time frustrated, disappointed, and depressed when we identify ourselves with them. Every pleasure and pain, success and failure, loss and gain affects us in one way or another, and we are tossed about by experiences which have little significance in the larger scheme of things.

We live in two different worlds and have no way of bridging the gulf between them. When we attempt to live in our inner world, we are distracted by worldly concerns. In the outer world we forget our spiritual goals, and when we remember them we condemn ourselves for our forgetfulness. In the deepest part of our being, however, we know that true happiness comes only from the realization that we are free from the cycle of birth and death. And we know that the greatest loss is to fail to reach that place before the body returns to dust.

The scriptures describe many sadhanas for overcoming this situation. Some can be followed as we keep ourselves active in the world. Some involve renouncing the world and all worldly concerns. But whatever path you follow, there are several key points to consider before you embark on the journey.

START FROM WHERE YOU ARE

Before you embark on any journey, you should be familiar with the map of your route and know exactly where you are on that map. How successful you are at reaching the nearest highway depends on how well you know your immediate locale as well as the surrounding terrain. On your spiritual journey, this means that you must know your temperament, your habit patterns, and your principal strengths and weaknesses before you commit to a spiritual practice. Scrutinize the part of your life that troubles you the most—the fatigue brought on by your job, or anxiety over unpaid bills, for example. You will not be able to escape all of your problems, but resolving them is as important as actually undertaking a practice.

Most problems are the result of not fulfilling your worldly duties and obligations, but you will not have the freedom of mind to attend to your spiritual practice until you do. One of the biggest mistakes aspirants make is committing themselves to spiritual practice as a means of escaping from their duties, but if you shun your duties you will have committed yourself to sadhana at a level you cannot sustain. This will be counterproductive in the long run.

You also need to be familiar with your physical capacity. According to the scriptures, the body is the basic instrument for spiritual development. Physical vitality is the key to progressing on the path, but physical pain, disease, and occasional illness are facts of life; they cannot be ignored or dissolved by mere philosophy. So you must design a practice that does not aggravate your physical problems, and vice versa. Begin by working within the limits of your current capacity, and then gradually work toward expanding it.

CHOOSE A PATH

Analyze your temperament and habits to determine your pro-
clivities. This will enable you to choose a specific aspect of yoga for
your main focus. If you are an intellectual, then *jñana* yoga (the
path of knowledge) will be the most effective one for you. If you are
emotional, you can transform your emotions into love and devotion
and attain union with God by following the path of *bhakti* yoga. If
you are healthy and have little interest in studying the scriptures,
sharpening your intellect, or purifying your emotions, then the path
of hatha yoga, under the guidance of a competent yogi, will be the
most fruitful. The path of karma yoga (the yoga of selfless action) is
suitable for you if you enjoy doing things for others and sharing the
fruits of your actions. And if your main interest lies in knowing
yourself at every level and awakening the infinite, dormant forces
within, then follow the path of kundalini yoga.

Regardless of which path you choose, you must begin with a
healthy body and a sound mind. For example, if you have a number
of beautifully tailored jackets, but are so ill or in such a bad mood
that you can't leave your bedroom, these jackets are useless.
Similarly, if you know a great deal about spiritual practices and have
been given practices by a competent teacher but have pain in your
knees or are distracted by memories and hopes each time you sit to
meditate, then these practices will have little effect.

Keeping your body and mind in good health requires following
a routine of proper exercise, breathing practices, relaxation, and a
systematic process of meditation. Some basic guidelines follow.

PHYSICAL EXERCISE

According to yoga science, the best exercises are those that
stimulate the whole body rather than just one particular muscle
group. Yoga postures stretch and stimulate the muscles, ligaments,
and joints, restoring elasticity and tone to the body. They stimulate
circulation and revitalize the internal organs, the brain, and the ner-

vous system. They enable the respiratory system to perform more efficiently by taking in greater amounts of oxygen and eliminating more toxins. They also increase resistance to fatigue and relieve tension. A session of yoga exercises should be designed so that exertion is balanced with rest and relaxation.

Yoga postures are not a substitute for aerobic exercise, however. Even during peak performance they don't alter normal functioning of the lungs and heart, and so they can be practiced by almost everyone. They are designed to create and maintain a healthy body and a peaceful mind. There are four key points to remember:

- Coordinate breath and movement. With each movement, pay attention to your breath; make sure that your physical movement does not interfere with your breathing pattern, and vice versa. Inhale each time the posture causes your chest to expand, and exhale when it contracts.
- Stay within your capacity. Be aware of your current level of strength, flexibility, and stamina. Stop before you feel fatigued. The object is to feel good—not only while you are exercising, but also after you are finished.
- Balance your routine. The stress on a particular limb, organ, or muscle group created by one exercise should be counterbalanced by another exercise. For example, the plow posture stretches the back of the neck and should be followed by the fish posture, which stretches the front of the neck.
- Relax. Begin and end each exercise session with a systematic relaxation.

Because yoga exercises work with the entire body, including the internal organs, the effects are subtle, so be careful not to do too much. It's best to start with twenty to thirty minutes of simple *asanas* and watch how your body responds as you include more advanced postures in your routine. Maintaining a regular, moderate practice and following it with a period of relaxation will enable you to improve your capacity in a delightful and amazing way. Your sense of enjoyment and how your body feels are the best indications of how much to exercise.

Traditionally morning is considered to be the best time for *asanas* because the stomach is empty, the colon is clean, and the atmosphere is calm and soothing. Because of stress and lack of proper rest, however, many people are stiff in the morning. And many are too busy in the morning to have a relaxed session. So, in the modern world evening may be a better time.

The main drawback to evening practice is that people are tired or jangled after a hectic day (or too full because they stopped off for a bite on the way home from work). So if you choose to practice in the evening, then make time for yourself by cutting down on other commitments, plan to eat lightly, and be sure to do a relaxation exercise before starting yoga postures.

Breathing Practices

The scriptures say that breath is life and life is breath. They say that breath is the link between the individual Self and the cosmic being and between body and mind. Through the breath, they say, the individual receives vitality from the atmosphere and remains connected with cosmic awareness. In other words, a healthy breathing pattern ensures the health of both body and mind. On the physical level the yoga breathing techniques are called *pranayama*, which literally means expanding the vital force, or gaining control over the activities of the vital force within. The following breathing exercises are especially suitable for us "modern" people.

diaphragmatic breathing

The diaphragm is the muscle that divides the torso into two separate chambers: the thorax and the abdomen. It forms the floor of the thorax and rests against the base of the lungs. As it relaxes during exhalation, this dome-shaped muscle presses against the lungs from below. Inhalation follows as the diaphragm contracts.

In a healthy person the movement of the diaphragm is responsible for seventy-five percent of the exchange of gases in the lungs. But the diaphragm is often tense, blocking natural breathing and causing fatigue, tension, and more serious problems. One of the first aims of yoga is to reestablish good breathing habits, and restoring the habit of diaphragmatic breathing accomplishes this effectively.

You can learn what diaphragmatic breathing feels like in the crocodile posture: Lie on your stomach with your legs a comfortable distance apart. The toes can be pointed in or out, whichever is more comfortable. Fold the arms in front of the body, resting the hands on the biceps. Position the arms so that the base of the rib cage touches the floor, as pictured.

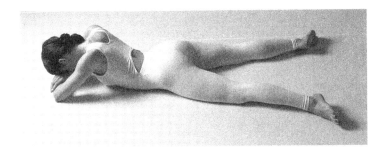

As you breathe in this position, the diaphragm moves vertically, pressing against the lungs from below. When you inhale, the abdomen expands, pressing against the floor, and the back gently rises. As you exhale, the abdomen contracts and the back gently falls. Both of these effects are produced by the movement of the diaphragm.

Establish the habit of diaphragmatic breathing in daily life, twenty-four hours a day. You can do this by practicing the crocodile pose twice a day for five to ten minutes. When you're finished, roll onto your back and observe your abdomen as it expands and contracts with the breath. Next, sit in a chair and again watch your breathing, keeping your abdomen relaxed. The last step is to continue to breathe diaphragmatically while you are standing. Practice regularly until diaphragmatic breathing becomes a habit.

The following checklist will help you evaluate your breathing:

- The breath flows smoothly.
- There is no pause between breaths.
- The breath flows silently.
- Exhalation and inhalation are approximately equal.
- The breath is deep, yet the upper chest barely moves.

Diaphragmatic breathing enables you to feel your best, gain emotional control and balance, and reduce fatigue and stress. The habit of diaphragmatic breathing is basic to all yoga breathing practices.

channel purification

Alternate nostril breathing, also known as channel purification, is a means of purifying the subtle energy channels in the body and bringing the activities of the nervous system to a state of balance.

Sit with your head, neck, and trunk erect so that your spine is balanced and steady and you can breathe freely. Gently close your eyes.

Breathe diaphragmatically. Let each exhalation and inhalation be the same length—smooth, slow, and relaxed. Do not allow the breath to be forced or jerky. With practice, the length of the breath will increase.

To begin the practice, close one nostril, then exhale and inhale smoothly and completely through the other. The inhalation and exhalation are of equal length and there is no sense of forcing the breath.

Now alternate sides, completing one full breath on the opposite side.

Continue alternating between the nostrils until you have completed a full round of the practice (three breaths on each side, for a total of six breaths). Then lower your hand and breathe gently and smoothly through both nostrils. For a deeper practice, complete two more rounds. (Note: When practicing three rounds in one sitting, the second of the three rounds begins on the opposite nostril, and the pattern of alternation is therefore the reverse of rounds one and three.)

two-to-one breathing

This breathing practice is an absolute necessity for those who live in cities where the air is polluted. It cleans the lungs and purifies the blood. The method is as follows.

First establish a pattern of even breathing (inhalation and exhalation are of equal duration). You may do this practice either in the corpse pose or in a sitting posture. You can mentally count to make sure your inhalation and exhalation are the same length.

After you have established a pattern of even breathing (it may take a few days or a couple of weeks), begin to lengthen the inhalation. You can accomplish this by counting to four while inhaling, for example, and to eight while exhaling. Once you have comfortably established the ratio of two-to-one breathing, stay at this level for a while. As you continue you will gradually eliminate the mental counting and maintain the 2:1 ratio by "feel."

Over time, advanced students may lengthen the duration of the breaths. You may set a goal of gradually increasing the length of the breaths to 10:5, 12:6, 14:7, and finally 16:8. A number of weeks or months of practice at each level will give you mastery.

relaxation

The word "relaxation" here may be misleading, for if you try to relax, you are bound to fail. Relaxation must be learned systematically and then allowed to progress naturally. In relaxation one learns the art of letting go.

There are many techniques for yoga relaxation. The following exercise forms the base from which many succeeding exercises may be learned. It relieves tension effectively and helps to bring the mind into a state of relaxed concentration.

Lie on your back. Use a thin cushion under your head. Cover your body with a sheet or thin shawl and place the legs a comfortable distance apart. The arms should be slightly separated from the body, the palms turned up. The spine should not be bent to either side. Take time to adjust your posture, and then become still. Close your eyes and be aware of the presence of your body, the space around you, and the place where your body rests. Observe your entire body from head to toe. Cultivate and enjoy its perfect stillness.

Now bring your attention to your breath. Observe each exhalation and inhalation and let the breath become deep and diaphragmatic. Breathing out, release all tension, waste, fatigue, and worry. Inhale a sense of energy and well-being. Do not pause between the breaths. Repeat this a few times. Next, gently survey your body mentally—you will release tension naturally in the places where you observe it. This process of "letting go" is the relaxation process. Move your awareness from the head to the toes and then back to the head, following this sequence:

forehead
eyebrows and eyes
nose*
cheeks
mouth
jaw
chin
neck
shoulders
upper arms
lower arms
hands
fingers
fingertips*
fingers
hands

lower arms

upper arms

shoulders

chest

heart center**

stomach

navel region

pelvic region

upper legs

lower legs

feet

toes**

At these places, you may pause for two or four** relaxed breaths when you are traveling from head to toe.

Now reverse the order and proceed upward, this time without any pauses.

Some practice will be required in order to complete this exercise without a lapse in your attention. If your mind wanders, gently bring it back to the relaxation process.

After progressing through the whole body, gently relax your mind. Turn your attention to the quiet flow of your breath. For a few minutes, rest and feel that this subtle stream of breath is a link joining you to the cosmos. You will be in harmony and at peace. Then roll onto your side and sit up.

concentration and meditation

To overcome fatigue before you sit for meditation, use a relaxation technique followed by alternate nostril breathing. Make a mental resolution that for the next twenty to thirty minutes you will entertain neither memories of the past nor thoughts of the future.

Sit crosslegged on the floor, or sit on a chair with your feet flat on the floor. Make sure that your head, neck, and trunk are aligned. Relax your shoulders and let your hands rest on your knees, thighs, or legs.

Breathe gently and naturally without jerks, pauses, or noise. Focus on your breath and watch how it flows from the tip of your nostrils to your heart center as you exhale, and from the heart center to the tip of your nostrils as you inhale.

After a few breaths, focus mentally on the sound "so hum." While you inhale listen to the sound "so," and while you exhale listen to the sound "hum." Let your mind, breath, and the sound "so hum" flow together. Stay with this practice for as long as you find it enjoyable.

If you have received a personal mantra through formal initiation you may focus on that mantra and follow the meditation instructions given to you. The instructions you receive personally supersede these general guidelines.

The Real Journey

Yoga exercises, breathing techniques, relaxation, and concentration on the breath prepare you for the spiritual journey, and after you have been practicing for a while you'll notice that to a great degree your body and mind will follow your instructions. The smooth and rhythmic flow of your breath will have helped you eliminate many obstacles and you will have a sense that a great joy lies deep within you. But so far you have not attained it.

In the beginning, meditating on the sound "so hum" is rewarding, but after a while you will reach a plateau. That is the time to look for direct and personal guidance. Experienced teachers can help you understand the exact nature of your personal sadhana, and they know how to introduce you to the teacher within so that you can keep receiving guidance without relying overtly on external teaching.

An authentic teacher will introduce you to the Divine by initiating you into a mantra, the divine word that in the beginning of creation was with God and was God. In Sanskrit literature this is called "mantra"; in other spiritual literature, it is called "nam." In the

Judeo-Christian tradition it is called "the Word."

A teacher will give you precise instruction in how to string the arrow of the mantra on the bow of the mind, and let the arrow fly at the moment your entire awareness is focused on the target. Then, as it penetrates the target, a multileveled mystery is unveiled. Self-realization, which is the purpose of life, is accomplished only after this takes place. Fear of the unknown vanishes and you are truly at peace. True knowledge dawns. And in the light of that knowledge neither present actions nor the actions of the past bind you anymore. Such a person is a *jivanmukta*—one who is liberated here and now.

Because the highest duty (Self-realization) has been accomplished, a *jivanmukta* is free from all other duties. But such enlightened souls do not become inactive. The eternal dance of the benign and beautiful divine force they experience within themselves manifests in their every thought, speech, and action. Their body and mind move spontaneously to perform actions for the benefit of their fellow beings. From their perspective, the actions they perform are virtually effortless because those actions are motivated and carried out by the will of the Divine.

Even when they withdraw themselves from the world and live in seclusion, these enlightened ones continue doing their sadhana, not because they have something yet to achieve but because they find delight in doing so. To keep discovering the subtle laws of the forces that control the manifest world is their recreation. They practice and gain knowledge of such highly evolved spiritual sciences as *pranavidya,* the science of prana; *daharavidya,* the science of the internal cave; *surya vijñana,* the science of the mystical sun; and *Sri Vidya,* the highest of all spiritual sciences.

From our everyday perspective, practicing spirituality might seem to be hard work. It requires taking care of our body, disciplining our senses (which they don't like), inducing the mind to turn inward (which it has forgotten how to do), and, finally, it places top priority on knowing Atman, the soul. To do this we have to let go of the past to live in the present, and we have to rid ourselves of worldly trash to enjoy the fragrance of the divine Self. But once we have accomplished that much, the journey becomes effortless. When we prepare ourselves, the enlightened ones—the *brahma rishis*—pull us up and place us on the highest summit.

As Swami Rama tells us: "Then the illumined practitioner sits calm in his celestial sessions with the highest of powers and drinks the wine of infinite beatitude. This child of immortality is a child of universal parents, protected all the time by the Mother Divine. And this rapturous child of bliss, intoxicated in delight, remains one with the Divine. He becomes a sage, a sleepless envoy and an ever-wakeful guide for those who tread the path. Such a leader on the path marches in front of human people, to comfort, help, and enlighten them."

Glossary

a b h a s a v a d a Reflectionism; a philosophical doctrine according-ing to which the material world is simply a reflection of what lies in the realm of pure consciousness. According to this theory, the absolute reality alone exists—the external world is mere appearance.

a b h y a s a Practice; a yogic term that refers to the process of making an effort to stay on one point, i.e., the object of meditation. Accomplishment in the practice is attained when one continues practicing for a long period of time without interruption.

a c h a r a h Healthy living; a code of conduct composed of guide-lines for healthy living.

a c h a r y a One whose example can be confidently followed in all areas of life; a teacher who has authority in a particular area of learning; a person well versed in spiritual texts; a spiritual teacher.

a d v a i t a Non-dual transcendental truth. According to Vedanta philosophy, behind all diversities there lies only one truth, called Brahman. It is due to ignorance that one sees duality, but as knowledge dawns, duality disappears and the aspirant realizes his or her oneness with the absolute truth.

a d v a i t a   b h a k t i The expression of divine love in which the lover and the beloved have become one; the state of ecstasy in which the devotee is completely merged in, and has become one with, the Divine.

a d v a i t a   V e d a n t a Non-dualistic school of Vedanta philosophy. There are several subschools of Vedanta—such as *dvaita,* which expounds dualism; *vishishta advaita,* which expounds qualified non-dualism, and so forth. Advaita Vedanta, taught by the sages of the *Upanishads,* is the foremost of the Vedanta schools.

a g h o r a   m a r g a One of the most esoteric spiritual paths. Literally *a* means "not," and *ghora* means "violent, destructive." This path leads to the realization of *aghora shakti,* the most benevolent and benign form of the divine force.

a g n i   v i d y a The esoteric science of fire.

a h a r a   s h u d d h i Purification of food. According to the scriptures not only the body but also our thinking processes are greatly affected by the food we eat. Therefore eating pure, fresh, nutritious, and light food in the right amounts, at the right time, with the right mental attitude is of utmost importance. Without observing a dietary discipline one cannot successfully work with oneself.

a h i m s a Non-violence; non-hurting; non-killing; the first and foremost among five restraints *(yamas)* mentioned in yoga literature.

a p a r a   b h a k t i *See* bhakti.

a p a r i g r a h a Non-possessiveness; one of the five restraints of yoga.

a s a n a Literally, the place to sit or the seat on which one sits; the meditative pose; the practice of postures.

a s h v a m e d h a The horse sacrifice. In the *Upanishads* it refers to the spiritual discipline in which one systematically learns how to tame the senses (the horses) and offer them to the fire of Brahman.

a t m a k r i p a *See* kripa.

a t m a s h a k t i The power of Atman; inner strength; also identified with *kundalini shakti.*

A t m a n The pure Self; pure consciousness. The Atman is the real Self, as opposed to ego, which identifies itself with the objects of the world.

a v a d h u t a One whose *vasanas* and *samskaras* have been completely washed off; an enlightened being who, due to her or his transcendence of the mundane level of awareness, remains oblivious to worldly norms.

a v i d y a Ignorance; lack of knowledge; mistaking one thing for something else; the primeval affliction—the mother of all other afflictions such as ego, attachment, aversion, and fear. It is overcome only by *vidya*, true knowledge, or the knowledge of the Self.

b h a k t i Devotion; unconditional love for the Divine. True love and devotion for the highest truth alone can uplift the consciousness of the aspirant. Through intense love and devotion for the Divine, an aspirant can attain the unitary experience, a state of highest delight. There are two levels of the experience of *bhakti:*

apara bhakti and *para bhakti*. *Apara bhakti* is the lower stage of *bhakti*, in which an aspirant feels that he or she is separate from the Beloved (God), and makes an effort to express love and devotion by actions such as singing the glory of God, chanting, worshipping, and so forth. However, when one becomes constantly aware of the presence of God, when every single thought, speech, and action is fully mingled with the awareness of God and an aspirant experiences unity with God, such a state is *para bhakti*—the highest state of *bhakti*. *Apara bhakti* refers to the process of loving God, whereas *para bhakti* refers to the state of awareness in which the adept simply remains inebriated in divine love.

b h a k t i   y o g a   The yoga of *bhakti*. The path of devotion.

b r a h m a c h a r i   Apprentice swami. One who dwells in Brahman consciousness; one who practices continence; one who is totally dedicated to the study of the *Vedas* and is not involved in secular, family life.

B r a h m a n   The all-pervading, eternal, absolute, non-dualistic truth.

b r a h m a n a   A particular portion of Vedic literature dedicated to rituals and ceremonies.

b r a h m a   n a d i   The most subtle *nadi*, which transcends even *sushumna*. It is through this *nadi* that a yogi goes beyond the *ajña* chakra and attains a particular state of *samadhi* called *unmani*, the state beyond mind. *See also* brahma-randhra.

b r a h m a - r a n d h r a   Literally, the hole of Brahman or the passage leading to Brahman; a particular *nadi*, also known as *brahma nadi*, situated between the *ajña* chakra and the *sahasrara* chakra.

brahmarishi The knower of Brahman; a seer; a realized soul.

buddhi The intellect; the faculty of reason and discernment.

chandra vidya Lunar science; the science of the mystical moon; also known as *soma vidya*. The first reference to this science is found in the tenth book of the *Rig Veda,* and is later elaborated in the *Upanishads* and tantric texts.

171

chitta Mind; mindfield. A generic term referring to all faculties of mind, such as *manas,* the lower mind; *ahankara,* ego; and *buddhi,* intellect. In some cases, *chitta* refers to the unconscious mind.

dahara vidya The spiritual science that leads to the realization of the pure space of consciousness.

dama Self-restraint; self-control; self-mastery; discipline of senses.

danda A staff that a renunciate carries all the time.

darshana Vision; direct realization, as opposed to the information gained through the senses; to have a glimpse of the real presence of the deity.

dashanami The ten renunciate traditions in addition to the five main monastic orders established by Shankaracharya.

deha vijñana The yogic science pertaining to deeper understanding of the human body and the subtle forces that regulate the functions of the body. This science deals not only with the physical structure of the body, such as muscular, skeletal, and neurological systems, but also with the pranic forces and the intricate *nadi* system.

d h a r m a   Duty; spiritual and ethical disciplines that are helpful for the growth of an individual as well as society.

d h u n i   The fire yogis prepare and constantly tend as part of their spiritual discipline.

g a y a t r i   m a n t r a   One of the best-known Vedic mantras; its name comes from the meter in which it is written.

g a y a t r i   p u r a s h c h a r a n a   A systematic practice of meditating on the *gayatri* mantra in a specific period of time.

g a y a t r i   s h a k t i   The power of the *gayatri* mantra; also known as *Savitri*.

g u n a s   The intrinsic forces of primordial nature, namely *sattva*, *rajas*, and *tamas*.

g u r u   Spiritual master.

g u r u d e v a   A way of referring to the guru with honor and respect.

g u r u   k r i p a   *See* kripa.

h a n s a   Swan; a term referring to accomplished yogis who live in the Himalayas, around and beyond Gangotri.

h a t h a   y o g a   The path of yoga consisting of the first four rungs of *raja* yoga: *yama, niyama, asana,* and *pranayama.*

h i m a - s a m a d h i   Casting off one's body in deep snow.

i c h c c h a   s h a k t i   The power of will; the primordial will of the Divine; the intrinsic power of consciousness; the creative power, followed by the power of knowledge and the power of action. The most profound study of *ichccha shakti* is found in *shaivist* and *Sri Vidya* schools of philosophy.

i s h t a   d e v a t a   One's chosen name and form of the Godhead.

i s h v a r a   k r i p a   *See* kripa.

j a l a - s a m a d h i   Casting off one's body in water.

j a l e b i   An Indian sweet.

j i v a   The individual self; the consciousness that identifies with body, senses, and mind, and as a result becomes a victim of pleasure and pain, birth and death.

j i v a n m u k t a   One who is liberated here and now; one who, due to an elevated state of knowledge, remains unaffected by the charms and temptations of the world and the pairs of opposites: pleasure and pain, loss and gain, success and failure.

j ñ a n a   y o g a   The yoga of knowledge. According to this school, it is through knowledge that one attains liberation, burns *samskaras*, and becomes free once and for all.

j ñ a n i   The knower of truth; one who has attained knowledge.

k a m a   Desire; an intrinsic aspect of divine will; the first step of the descent of consciousness toward manifestation of the material world.

k a m a   k a l a   Primordial desire, the power of will *(ichccha shakti);* in *tantra shastra* it refers to the triangle and the forces symbolized by the triangle.

k a m a n d a l u   Water vessel; traditional water pot that *sadhus* carry.

k a r m a   y o g a   The yoga of action.

k a r u n a   Compassion; the unconditional love of the Divine for all individual souls.

k r i p a   Grace; a favor; divine help. According to the yogic texts the most subtle hurdles are removed by divine grace, which usually descends after the aspirant has made the utmost effort. The full advantage of this divine grace is achieved when the fourfold "graces" meet. They are: *shastra kripa,* the grace of the scriptures; *atma kripa,* the grace of one's Self; *guru kripa,* the grace of the guru; and *Ishvara kripa,* the grace of God.

k u n d a l i n i   y o g a   The path of yoga where one finds a systematic method of awakening the dormant force and leading it step by step to the *sahasrara,* the highest center of consciousness.

l a k s h m a n a   r e k h a   The line drawn by Lakshmana, the younger brother of Rama, the hero of the Ramayana. It is a line of demarcation that is supposedly charged with a protective spiritual energy, so that an aspirant doing *sadhana* inside the boundary remains free of all obstacles that originate outside the line.

l i l a   Divine play; the play of the divine force that manifests in the form of the creation, maintenance, and annihilation of the universe.

m a h a   m a y a   The highest creative force; the intrinsic power of Brahman.

m a h a   p u r a s h c h a r a n a   A grand spiritual undertaking; in the case of meditation on the *gayatri* mantra, a *maha purashcharana* would consist of repeating the mantra 2,400,000 times within a defined period of time, (e.g., 16 months or 32 months). Strict disciplines related to diet, silence, refraining from socializing, sleeping moderately, and so forth, go along with this practice.

m a h a v i d y a (s) The great knowledge, or the great spiritual paths; the ten main esoteric paths in the yoga tradition of *shakti sadhana:* Kali, Tara, Chhinnamasta, Sodashi (Sri Vidya), Matangi, Tripura-bhairavi, Bhuvaneshvari, Bagalamukhi, Kamala, and Dhumavati.

m a n a n a Pondering; contemplating.

m a n d a l a The visual depiction of the personified form of a mantra; a visible depiction of the invisible forces of nature, as well as different aspects of the human psyche. A thorough knowledge of myths and symbols is necessary to grasp the essence of a mandala.

m a y a The creative force of Brahman. *See also* maha maya.

M i m a m s a A system of philosophy that evolved from the *Vedas* and emphasizes ritual.

m o k s h a k a m j ñ a n a m The knowledge that liberates.

m u m u k s h a Desire for liberation. One of the qualities a student of *jñana* yoga must cultivate before the study of the scriptures and contemplation can become a means to spiritual unfoldment.

n a d a The eternal sound yogis hear during meditation.

n i d i d h y a s a n a Applying knowledge that one has gained from the study and deep contemplation of the scriptures.

p a n d i t A learned person; a Sanskrit scholar; one who has access to ancient scriptures. Ideally, a pandit is one whose actions are not motivated by personal whims and who has burnt the seeds of all karmas in the fire of knowledge.

p a r a b h a k t i *See* bhakti.

p a r a v i d y a The highest knowledge.

p a r a k a y a p r a v e s h a An advanced technique of yoga that enables a yogi to cast off the body at will and acquire another body as he or she chooses.

p a r i v r a j a k a A monk who has no permanent residence, possesses nothing, and continually travels from place to place.

p r a k r i t i The primordial cause of the universe; nature.

p r a n a The life-force.

p r a n a v i d y a The science of prana, the vital force.

p r a n a y a m a Control over and expansion of the vital force; breathing exercises.

p r a t i b i m b a v a d a Reflectionism. *See also* abhasa vada.

p r a t y a h a r a Withdrawal of the senses; the fifth of the eight rungs in the ladder of *raja* yoga.

r a j a y o g a The royal path; the path of yoga in which the entire practices described in eight steps: yama, niyama, asana, pranayama, pratyahara, dharana, dhyana, samadhi.

r i s h i   A seer; a knower of the truth; a sage to whom a mantra or a group of mantras is revealed.

s a d g u r u   A genuine spiritual master, as opposed to the teachers from whom one gathers information on diverse subjects; a spiritual master capable of purifying a student's heart and opening the spiritual eye.

s a d h a k a   A spiritual aspirant; a seeker.

s a d h a n a   Spiritual practice.

s a d h u   Saint; one who has dedicated their life to spiritual pursuit. A wandering monk.

s a m a d h a n a   Putting together or arranging in proper order; putting the teachings of different teachers and scriptures in proper context.

s a m a d h i   State of tranquility; state of mind where there are no thought constructs.

s a m a y a   One of the three stages or schools of tantra yoga. *See also* tantra.

s a m s k a r a s   Subtle impressions of past deeds.

s a n k a l p a   Determination.

s a n k a l p a   s h a k t i   The power of determination.

s a n n y a s a   The path of renunciation.

s a n n y a s i n   One who has taken the vows of renunciation.

s a t s a n g a   The company of a wise person.

s a t t v a   One of the attributes of nature; the energy that tends to move upward and is light and bright; the force of illumination.

s a t t v i c   Pertaining to uplifting thoughts, feelings, and energies, pure in quality and behavior.

s h a k t i   Power; force; energy.

s h a k t i p a t a   The bestowing of spiritual energy; the descent of divine grace; transmission of spiritual wisdom.

s h a k t i s m   The school of philosophy that advocates the supremacy of shakti. The philosophy that claims the whole world evolves from shakti and that, even in its manifest form, the world exists in the realm of shakti and ultimately dissolves back into shakti.

s h a s t r a   k r i p a   *See* kripa.

s h r a v a n a   Listening to scriptures or teachers; the first step in the Vedantic method of *sadhana*.

s h r o t r i y a   b r a h m i n   One who is well versed in the *Vedas* and lives up to the Vedic injunctions.

s i d d h a s a n a   The accomplished pose; one of the traditional meditative *asanas*.

S r i   V i d y a   The highest among all spiritual sciences; the culmination of all the philosophical, metaphysical, and spiritual wis dom of the ancient sages. According to this system of thought, all that exists in the macrocosm also exists in the microcosm. It is in this school of yoga that one finds a profound discussion of yantra, mantra, chakras, and kundalini shakti.

s t h a l a - s a m a d h i   Casting off one's body while sitting in *siddhasana.*

s u r y a   v i j ñ a n a   The mystical science of the sun; solar science; the science pertaining to exploring the source of the life-force.

s v a d h y a y a   Self-study; study of scriptures as well as study of one's self at every level.

s v a r a   v i j ñ a n a   The science of breath; the science of pranic force.

t a n t r a   A school of yoga which maps the spiritual journey in three stages: kaula, mishra, and samaya. In the kaula stage, one learns a system of using all external objects as means for spiritual unfoldment. At the mishra level, the external means are not yet abandoned, but focus shifts to practice of internal methods of meditation. At the samaya level, the practitioner is no longer involved in external, ritualistic practices but practices only the internal methods and learns the system of meditating at the *sahasrara,* the crown chakra.

t a p a s   Austerity; the method of yogic disciplines that help one balance the energies of the body *(vata, pitta,* and *kapha);* enduring the pairs of opposites (pleasure and pain, attraction and aversion, hot and cold, etc.).

t i t i k s h a   Forbearance; tolerance; endurance.

t i v r a   m u m u k s h a   A strong desire for liberation, as opposed to mere curiosity.

U p a n i s h a d s   A group of ancient scriptures, which are studied while sitting at the feet of the master. The great philosopher and yogi Shankaracharya wrote commentaries on eleven *Upanishads*, which are considered to be the principal ones.

u p a r a t i   Desisting from sensual pleasures; withdrawal of the senses so that one is not driven by temptations of the world; overcoming cravings for worldly pleasures.

v a i r a g y a   Non-attachment; remaining unaffected by the charms and temptations of the world; keeping the mind free from the worldly stains.

v a s a n a s   The subtle impressions of past deeds that influence the actions that we perform in the present; habit patterns; innate tendencies of the mind; subtle personality traits.

V e d a s   The world's most ancient scriptures, which contain the wisdom of the ancient sages. According to Indian tradition every single word of the *Vedas* was revealed to the *rishis* while meditating. They are not the works of human authors.

V e d a n t a   The culmination of Vedic wisdom; the last phase of Vedic literature; the philosophy that expounds the theory of non-dualism.

v i c h a r a   Right thinking; contemplation; discrimination; contemplative wisdom.

v i d y a   Spiritual science. Knowledge.

yajñopavita The sacred ceremonial thread that students of the *Vedas* receive when they begin their studies.

yantra Geometrical diagram giving a visual understanding of invisible forces of nature; a geometrical figure laden with symbolic meanings, often used as an object of concentration.

About Pandit Rajmani Tigunait

PANDIT RAJMANI TIGUNAIT, PHD, is a modern-day master and living link in the unbroken Himalayan Tradition. He embodies the yogic and tantric wisdom which the Himalayan Tradition has safeguarded for thousands of years. Pandit Tigunait is the successor of Sri Swami Rama of the Himalayas and the spiritual head of the Himalayan Institute. As a young man he committed himself to arduous spiritual practice and studied with renowned adepts of India before being initiated into the lineage of the Himalayan Tradition by his master, Sri Swami Rama, in 1976.

Pandit Tigunait is fluent in Vedic and Classical Sanskrit and holds two doctorates, one from the University of Allahabad (India), and another from the University of Pennsylvania. As a leading voice of YogaInternational.com and the author of 15 books, his teachings span a wide range, from scholarly analysis and scripture translation to practical guidance on applying yogic wisdom to modern life. Over the past 35 years, Pandit Tigunait has touched innumerable lives around the world as a teacher, guide, author, humanitarian, and visionary spiritual leader.

![HIMALAYAN INSTITUTE]

The main building of the Himalayan Institute headquarters near Honesdale, Pennsylvania

The Himalayan Institute

A leader in the field of yoga, meditation, spirituality, and holistic health, the Himalayan Institute is a nonprofit international organization dedicated to serving humanity through educational, spiritual, and humanitarian programs. The mission of the Himalayan Institute is to inspire, educate, and empower all those who seek to experience their full potential.

Founded in 1971 by Swami Rama of the Himalayas, the Himalayan Institute and its varied activities and programs exemplify the spiritual heritage of mankind that unites East and West, spirituality and science, ancient wisdom and modern technology.

Our international headquarters is located on a beautiful 400-acre campus in the rolling hills of the Pocono Mountains of northeastern Pennsylvania. Our spiritually vibrant community and peaceful setting provide the perfect atmosphere for seminars and retreats, residential programs, and holistic health services. Students from all over the world join us to attend diverse programs on subjects such as hatha yoga, meditation, stress reduction, ayurveda, and yoga and tantra philosophy.

In addition, the Himalayan Institute draws on roots in the yoga tradition to serve our members and community through the following programs, services, and products:

Mission Programs

The essence of the Himalayan Institute's teaching mission flows from the timeless message of the Himalayan Masters, and is echoed in our on-site mission programming. Their message is to first become aware of the reality within ourselves, and then to build a bridge between our inner and outer worlds.

Our mission programs express a rich body of experiential wisdom and are offered year-round. They include seminars, retreats, and professional certifications that bring you the best of an authentic yoga tradition, addressed to a modern audience. Join us on campus for our Mission Programs to find wisdom from the heart of the yoga tradition, guidance for authentic practice, and food for your soul.

Wisdom Library and Mission Membership

The Himalayan Institute online Wisdom Library curates the essential teachings of the living Himalayan Tradition. This offering is a unique counterpart to our in-person Mission Programs, empowering students by providing online learning resources to enrich their study and practice outside the classroom.

Our Wisdom Library features multimedia blog content, livestreams, podcasts, downloadable practice resources, digital courses, and an interactive Seeker's Forum. These teachings capture our Mission Faculty's decades of study, practice, and teaching experience, featuring new content as well as the timeless teachings of Swami Rama and Pandit Rajmani Tigunait.

We invite seekers and students of the Himalayan Tradition to become a Himalayan Institute Mission Member, which grants unlimited access to the Wisdom Library. Mission Membership offers a way for you to support our shared commitment to service, while deepening your study and practice in the living Himalayan Tradition.

Spiritual Excursions

Since 1972, the Himalayan Institute has been organizing pilgrimages for spiritual seekers from around the world. Our spiritual excursions follow the traditional pilgrimage routes where adepts of the Himalayas lived and practiced. For thousands of years, pilgrimage has been an essential part of yoga sadhana, offering spiritual seekers the opportunity to experience the transformative power of living shrines of the Himalayan Tradition.

Global Humanitarian Projects

The Himalayan Institute's humanitarian mission is yoga in action—offering spiritually grounded healing and transformation to the world. Our humanitarian projects serve impoverished communities in India, Mexico, and Cameroon through rural empowerment and environmental regeneration. By putting yoga philosophy into practice, our programs are empowering communities globally with the knowledge and tools needed for a lasting social transformation at the grassroots level.

Publications

The Himalayan Institute publishes over 60 titles on yoga, philosophy, spirituality, science, ayurveda, and holistic health. These include the best-selling books *Living with the Himalayan Masters* and *The Science of Breath*, by Swami Rama; *The Power of Mantra and the Mystery of Initiation, From Death to Birth, Tantra Unveiled,* and two commentaries on the *Yoga Sutra—The Secret of the Yoga Sutra: Samadhi Pada* and *The Practice of the Yoga Sutra: Sadhana Pada—* by Pandit Rajmani Tigunait, PhD; and the award-winning *Yoga: Mastering the Basics* by Sandra Anderson and Rolf Sovik, PsyD. These books are for everyone: the interested reader, the spiritual novice, and the experienced practitioner.

PureRejuv Wellness Center

For over 40 years, the PureRejuv Wellness Center has fulfilled part of the Institute's mission to promote healthy and sustainable lifestyles. PureRejuv combines Eastern philosophy and Western medicine in an integrated approach to holistic health—nurturing balance and healing at home and at work. We offer the opportunity to find healing and renewal through on-site wellness retreats and individual wellness services, including therapeutic massage and bodywork, yoga therapy, ayurveda, biofeedback, natural medicine, and one-on-one consultations with our integrative medical staff.

Total Health Products

The Himalayan Institute, the developer of the original Neti Pot, manufactures a health line specializing in traditional and modern ayurvedic supplements and body care. We are dedicated to holistic and natural living by providing products using non-GMO components, petroleum-free biodegrading plastics, and eco-friendly packaging that has the least impact on the environment. Part of every purchase supports our Global Humanitarian projects, further developing and reinforcing our core mission of spirituality in action.

For further information about our programs, humanitarian projects, and products:

call: 800.822.4547

e-mail: info@HimalayanInstitute.org

write: The Himalayan Institute
952 Bethany Turnpike
Honesdale, PA 18431

or visit: HimalayanInstitute.org

We are grateful to our members for their passion and commitment to share our mission with the world. Become a Mission Member and inherit the wisdom of a living tradition.

HIMALAYAN INSTITUTE®

inherit the wisdom of a living tradition tod

As a Mission Member, you will gain exclusive access to our online Wisdom Library. The Wisdom Library includes monthly livestream workshops, digital practicums and eCourses, monthly podcasts with Himalayan Institute Mission Faculty, and multimedia practice resources.

Mission Membership Benefi

- Never-before-seen content from Swami Rama & Pandit Tigunait
- New content announcements & weekly blog roundup
- Unlimited access to online yoga classes and meditation classes
- Members only digital workshops and monthly livestreams
- Downloadable practice resources and Prayers of the Tradition

Wisdom Library

Netra Tantra: Harnessing the Healing Force (Part 1)
Pandit Rajmani Tigunait, PhD | September 28, 2017
Read more

• • •

Get FREE access to the Wisdom Library for 30 days!

Mission Membership is an invitation to put your spiritual values into action by supporting our shared commitment to service while deepening your study and practice in the living Himalayan Tradition.

BECOME A MISSION MEMBER AT.
himalayaninstitute.org/mission-membership

LIVING WITH THE
HIMALAYAN
MASTERS

SWAMI RAMA

In this classic spiritual autobiography, hear the message of
Sri Swami Rama, one of the greatest sages of the 20th century.
As he shares precious experiences with his beloved master,
Sri Bengali Baba, and many other well-known and hidden
spiritual luminaries, you will have a glimpse of the living
tradition of the Himalayan Masters.

This spiritual treasure records Swami Rama's personal quest
for enlightenment and gives profound insights into the living
wisdom that is the core of his spiritual mission and legacy.
This living wisdom continues to enlighten seekers even
today, long after Swamiji's maha-samadhi in 1996, sharing
the timeless blessing of the sages of the Himalayan Tradition.

To order: 800-822-4547
Email: mailorder@HimalayanInstitute.org
Visit: HimalayanInstitute.org

The Secret of the Yoga Sutra
Samadhi Pada
Pandit Rajmani Tigunait, PhD

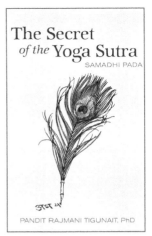

The Yoga Sutra is the living source wisdom of the yoga tradition, and is as relevant today as it was 2,200 years ago when it was codified by the sage Patanjali. Using this ancient yogic text as a guide, we can unlock the hidden power of yoga, and experience the promise of yoga in our lives. By applying its living wisdom in our practice, we can achieve the purpose of life: lasting fulfillment and ultimate freedom.

Paperback, 6" x 9", 331 pages
$24.95, ISBN 978-0-89389-277-7

The Practice of the Yoga Sutra
Sadhana Pada
Pandit Rajmani Tigunait, PhD

In Pandit Tigunait's practitioner-oriented commentary series, we see this ancient text through the filter of scholarly understanding and experiential knowledge gained through decades of advanced yogic practices. Through *The Secret of the Yoga Sutra* and *The Practice of the Yoga Sutra*, we receive the gift of living wisdom he received from the masters of the Himalayan Tradition, leading us to lasting happiness.

Paperback, 6" x 9", 389 Pages
$24.95, ISBN 978-0-89389-279-1

To order: 800-822-4547
Email: mailorder@HimalayanInstitute.org
Visit: HimalayanInstitute.org

HIMALAYAN
INSTITUTE®

Touched by Fire
Pandit Rajmani Tigunait, PhD

This vivid autobiography of a remarkable spiritual leader—Pandit Rajmani Tigunait, PhD—reveals his experiences and encounters with numerous teachers, sages, and his master, the late Swami Rama of the Himalayas. His well-told journey is filled with years of disciplined study and the struggle to master the lessons and skills passed to him. *Touched by Fire* brings Western culture a glimpse of Eastern philosophies in a clear, understandable fashion, and provides numerous photographs showing a part of the world many will never see for themselves.

Paperback with flaps, 6" x 9", 296 pages
$16.95, ISBN 978-0-89389-239-5

At the Eleventh Hour
Pandit Rajmani Tigunait, PhD

This book is more than the biography of a great sage—it is a revelation of the many astonishing accomplishments Swami Rama achieved in his life. These pages serve as a guide to the more esoteric and advanced practices of yoga and tantra not commonly taught or understood in the West. And they bring you to holy places in India, revealing why these sacred sites are important and how to go about visiting them. The wisdom in these stories penetrates beyond the power of words.

Paperback with flaps, 6" x 9", 448 pages
$18.95, ISBN 978-0-89389-211-1

To order: 800-822-4547
Email: mailorder@HimalayanInstitute.org
Visit: HimalayanInstitute.org

Perennial Psychology of the Bhagavad Gita
Swami Rama

With the guidance and commentary of Himalayan Master Swami Rama, you can explore the wisdom of the Bhagavad Gita, which allows one to be vibrant and creative in the exter nal world while maintaining a state of inner tranquility. This commentary on the Bhagavad Gita is a unique opportunity t see the Gita through the perspective of a master yogi, and is excellent version for practitioners of yoga meditation. Spiritu seekers, psychotherapists, and students of Eastern studies wil all find a storehouse of wisdom in this volume.

Paperback, 6" x 9", 479 pages
$19.95, ISBN 978-0-89389-090-2

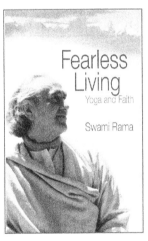

Fearless Living: Yoga and Faith
Swami Rama

Learn to live without fear—to trust a higher power, a divine purpose. In this collection of anecdotes from the astonishin life of Swami Rama, you will understand that there is a way to move beyond mere faith and into the realm of personal revelation. Through his astonishing life experiences we learn about ego and humility, see how to overcome fears that inhil us, discover sacred places and rituals, and learn the importan of a one-pointed, positive mind. Swami Rama teaches us to see with the eyes of faith and move beyond our self-imposed limitations.

Paperback with flaps, 6" x 9", 160 pages
$12.95, ISBN 978-0-89389-251-7

To order: 800-822-4547
Email: mailorder@HimalayanInstitute.org
Visit: HimalayanInstitute.org

HIMALAYAN
INSTITUTE®